BIG TALK
SMALL WALK
SMALL TALK
BIG WALK

A Walk to be Remembered

By

Mitzey Powers

Copyright © 2013 Mitzey Powers

All Rights Reserved. This book or any portion thereof may not be produced or used in any manner whatsoever without the express written permission of the publisher except for the use of brief quotations in the book review.

Printed in the United States of America

First Printing, 2013

ISBN 978-0-99-10373-1-5

Published at Amazon.com
www.amazon.com

Book design by Mitzey Powers
Book photography by Mitzey Powers and Jonathan Brooks
Book cover and book layout by Robert Kauffman
Book editing by Mike Valentino

This book is a work of non-fiction and thoroughly based on actual events and experiences in my life. Some names and places have been changed out of respect and protection.

Dedication

For my incredible husband Tom...
For loving me so deeply, unconditionally and securely that our bond grows dearer with each new step we take. Your desire to have me as your wife for the rest of your life, prompted you to get my plane ticket and purchase your own guidebook so you could follow my journey with me. You supported me in walking throughout Europe on the Camino de Santiago alone, so that I could unplug, de-stress and regain my footing. In your selflessness, I returned to you three months later, 76-pounds lighter and leaner, peaceful, joyful, clear-thinking and with a brain tumor that had nearly disappeared during my walk. Detaching from the daily stressors and tapping into God, nature and myself made me healthier than ever. In short, you gave me the freedom to do what I had to do for me. In turn, the gift you really gave me was the gift of my life. Now you find yourself with what you wanted most; spending the rest of your life with me. You're a man of small talk, Tom, but your walk through life is one of grace, love, mercy, forgiveness, strength, compassion and passion. I thank you for the amazing example you are to our three children and how you lovingly and joyfully picked up the pieces of another man's errors. I find it incredible how two grown men can walk such vastly different walks... one self-centeredly distracted by every vice known to man, no matter who gets hurts along his journey, and the other who chooses to walk the path of dignity, integrity, honor, God-centeredness, patience, love, forgiveness and loyalty. I adore you, Tom, and thank God for you in our lives! This is my chance to give back to you...

Sometimes when you let go of that which you desire to hold the tightest, you find yourself holding that which you desire the most!

For my children JB and Lindsay... because you both inspire me to be the best **ME** I can be!

I pray you always **DREAM BIG, THINK BIG, WALK BIG** and talk small!

You are my joy in life and I love you both...

For my Stepson Michael… I dearly love you! I am proud of the strong man you've become and am honored to have you in my life. Thank you for sharing your Dad with me, JB and Lindsay.

For my family of origin because without you, I would have never learned what NOT to do—

For my family of choice (including you Dad) because without you, I would have never learned what the true definition of family is.

Lastly, for you Mama. Heaven took you home when I was young but I thank you for being so strong, brave and courageous in your fight for living life and survival. The last few weeks with you made so many things right. Thank you for that gift of healing, Mom. Each time I see a butterfly, I always say "Hi Mama… I love you too." Enjoy your walks on streets of gold.

Parts

The Early Walk 1

The Lost Walk 21

The New Walk 89

BIG TALK 177

BIG WALK 195

BIG WALK…
BIG TALK ! 307

Acknowledgments

Dear God,
Without you I wouldn't have survived to this point; let alone thrived. With you ALL things are possible ! I give you the glory for who I am, all that I accomplish and all that I have. Thank you for loving me even when I'm not very lovable.

I thank my soul sister M K for DREAMING BIG, TALKING BIG AND WALKING BIG! You lead the way for others to do the same! I love you and wouldn't have had the courage to break free of my bondage without your belief! We are "functional" sisters by choice and for life!

I thank my children JB and Lindsay for growing into amazing young adults that make your dad and I look good. Without your strong wills, sense of adventure and complete and utter belief in me, this journey would never have taken place. Thank you for your short-term sacrifice; may you always see, feel and live the long-term gain!

I thank Betty Marvin (the wife of Pastor John Marvin) for being a strong woman of grace, love and integrity. You were always there for me as a child and throughout high school. You are an incredible example of a good-hearted, God-centered, integrity-filled woman that showed me that what matters most is not how others treat you, but how you handle it and treat them in return. Even though you were unaware of the abuse I was enduring as a child, you WALKED THE TALK... THANK YOU on behalf of all young people that your example has touched and influenced over the years. I am the woman, wife and mother that I am today directly because of your walking influence. I will always love and appreciate you!

I thank those at Pacific Garden Mission in downtown Chicago for their dedication to their inner-city ministry. You poured into me many years ago and now the walk continues as I pour into the lives of others.

I thank Charles, the doorman at the Knickerbocker Hotel in downtown Chicago. Many years ago, I passed by daily only to hear you say "Good morning, Miss Michelle… you know, someday you're gonna stay in this here highfalutin hotel!" It was a joy of my life to see you six years ago as you were retiring! Charles, you were right! I returned and stayed in that glorious hotel; just to see you again my friend! Thank you! You were the first person in my life that taught me to THINK BIG! Little things, many times, have the biggest impact!

I thank Maria and Paxti; owners of Casa Victoria, located in Ciruena Spain. My walk would have ended without you. You encouraged me without ever speaking a word of English! Kindness and love is a universal language that you both speak with ease. Your pension' was my oasis in the desert. Su dedicacion a los peregrinos es un hermoso paseo de su propio (Your dedication to pilgrims is a beautiful walk of your own) Te amo queridos amigos. (I love you dear friends!)

I thank those that followed my journey throughout Europe. I started the journey for me, but finished it for you! Your emails and messages kept me going. How is it that I was doing something that you all said that you couldn't? Your lack of belief in yourself led me to quickly realize that I had to finish in order to break that belief barrier for you!

Lastly, I thank Joseph Dirsa - Owner and innkeeper of the August Seven Inn in Daytona Beach FL. You put up with me for nine nights while I sequestered myself to write the book and it would not be what it is without the influences of you and your inn. You poured your soul into making your space a tender, special place of visual interest and aromas to incite feeling and thought. Every weary traveler should experience your inn.

Preface

This book was birthed out of heavenly harassment and the compulsion to call for a thought revolution. As a mental health professional, I learned that we, as adults, are products of patterns we learn in childhood... patterns that we are destined to repeat, until there is an interruption in our thinking and behavior. My patterns of mistrust of humanity grew into a total loss of faith; not in God, but in God's People. Stemming from abuse and misuse by legalistic authority figures, and family members as a child, through to adulthood with a handful of college degrees, an abusive ex-husband and two small children; one of which was severely disabled. Thankfully, my life was sprinkled with a few good intentioned people that walked the talk but most were self-consumed users of others. I found myself surrounded by narcissistic people that seemed to sense the fragrance of my giving spirit and feed on me until I ran dry. Why can't I say no ? Why can't I tell others to stop dumping their junk in my trash can; can't they see it's full. Why do I over commit? Why do I allow others to just plain use me up? The stress and distress of my everyday reality began to take a toll and I saw my health eroding before my very eyes. This vicious cycle seemed to be un-ending until my doctor told me that I needed to unplug my computer or it was going to crash. My mortality was staring me in the face and the veil of innocence was lifted! No more overlooking my needs! That was the interruption in my thinking that I needed and I had a thought revival ! I took drastic steps to change my thinking, my behavior, my health and it worked ! Having the courage to change began to inspire others to do the same. I was not expecting my journey to reveal as many things as it did... I didn't expect such a drastic change in the quiet recesses of my mind... I didn't expect to laugh so much... or realize all of the parallels in life, business, relationships and the deep paradigm shift that would occur... I didn't expect my journey to impact the walks of others... <u>but it has</u> ! If this obese, unfit, middle-aged, living in fear girl with a brain tumor can walk 2,000+ miles through Europe backpacking alone and change my life... then anyone can change their walk through life! I went from a wounded girl to a healthy, strong and powerful woman; I am woman... hear me roar ! It all starts with an interruption in your thinking and behavior. May my heart and experiences poured out amongst the pages of this book, be the interruption that you need! I pray that my BIG walk and small talk, inspires you to change yours!

Intro

From childhood to victimhood... to adulthood.
From wifehood to motherhood... to neighborhood.
From livelihood to falsehood... to sisterhood.
From selfhood to Godhood... to servanthood.

Living vs. dying
Honesty vs. denial
Courage vs. fear
Identity vs. roles
Possibilities vs. limitations
Chain-link vs. brick wall
Better vs. bitter
Kindness vs. indifference
We vs. me
Victor vs. victim
Walk vs. talk

Facing eroding health and my own mortality, which was directly related to choices I made in my daily life, I chose change. Why is it that it takes a drastic catalyst to spark major shifts in our lives? I had no choice but to honestly and thoroughly evaluate my life and make some changes FAST. As my doctor put it, I had to unplug or it was going to crash! What does that mean? How do I unplug? There is a price to pay for taking a sabbatical; financially and in my relationships. Is my life worth the price? I read a book in college about the Camino de Santiago; a highly held Christian pilgrimage throughout Europe that ends in Santiago de Compostelle, Spain. For thousands of years pilgrims would walk the Camino paths in search of finding God. All along the journey were others that dedicated their lives to working with and helping the pilgrims during their walk. I knew this was where I wanted to "unplug" and disappear to but who am I to think that I can do this? That was my intention but two days into it, my reasons changed... After three months of backpacking through Europe alone... 2,000+ miles of walking... *I had changed! I had a thought revival!* What led me to the walk, through the walk and what did I bring home with me. ... Buckle your seatbelt and prepare for a read that will provoke thought, self-evaluation and hopefully... a "thought revival"!

A better world begins with the shifting of one man's thinking!

Patterns and pathology. We all have them, learned them as a child and are destined to repeat them like a record that is stuck playing the same song until something interrupts it. Don't think for a second you are beyond this reality... you're not! Shifting your surroundings and those in it, starts with shifting you. A better world begins with the shifting of one man's thinking. What led me to lose my faith in God's people and humanity in general and what brought me to the realization that I was not beyond needing to honestly look at my life through new eyes. The world is filled with people that talk big and walk small. People that hold titles in leadership and others that are the followers; yet on both sides of the coin there is a general running thread of "get ahead". Using others to further yourself... using "God" to manipulate others, so as to line your pockets; the "me" mentality. Others talk a good talk but walk in judgment, criticism, condemnation or competition of their fellow man. Then you find those that have hearts of helping others so that the sense of being needed elevates their self-esteem, confidence and worth... These are those that get used up, manipulated and abused but are still all about getting ahead. Few and far between are the truly healthy, loving, genuine people that talk small but WALK BIG! They walk in a place of integrity, character, love, peace, honesty, compassion and are there to serve. Not to be walked upon but to be walked with. My story has them all.

PART 1

The Early Walk

CHAPTER 1

My story begins as yours… in my childhood.

On a lovely mild November morning, a beautiful little baby girl entered this world, as the newest citizen of Midwest America. I was born into a family with extremely legalistic religious views. My mother was "in menopause", so the doctor had told her, but nine months later I graced their presence and life as they knew it soon changed. I was the youngest of three, arriving nearly twenty years after my two siblings. So from the beginning of my life, dynamics were interesting to say the least.

I have vivid childhood memories, many of them disturbing and shrouded in secrecy. Why have I chosen to reveal them now? Feelings buried alive do not die. They just become splinters of the heart that fester over time, create patterns of bad behavior and result in infection that spreads to others. In my process of healing, the wounds had to be lanced, splinters removed, and the infection cleaned out. I also needed a strong dose of sharing, the only medicine for such deep psychological pain.

In order to understand the full scope of my walk into healthiness, I must speak the truth of what led me to the decision for change. We all have experiences in our childhood that influence and mold us into who we are as adults. Our parents merely repeated the patterns and pathology that they grew up with. Bad behavior does not mean bad people.

Spare the rod and spoil the child, considered sage advice at the time, represented but the least of my nightmarish memories. The razor strap and keen switch beatings were commonplace, not because I was a bad child but because my father seemed to always harbor this rage just beneath the surface and I seemed to be masterful at setting him off. My mother was just as good at manipulating me, through playing on my father's anger. If I did something she didn't approve of, I'd pay because she'd tell Daddy when he got home. I still, to this day, can recall the sly look on her face as he would grab my arm and firmly direct me to the basement. I learned at a young age to please my mother, at any cost, to avoid pain. Acceptance and approval came from pleasing and meeting the needs of others. As a child, I never felt loved by my mother (even though I couldn't seem to figure out why) but interestingly enough, I did my father. At times, I would wonder why he was so angry at me. What did I do that would make him so full of rage. Little did I realize, as a small child, that his anger and rage had nothing to do with me. I was just the recipient of it.

My siblings both married and left home within a few years of my birth but continued to live close by within the same town.

They both seem to have broken free of the religious limitations they were raised with and had created lives of their own. My sister attempted to build a loving relationship with me but within a few years it became clear that her choices in life resulted in a time of abuse and discord within her home. My contact with her was limited by my parents, supposedly to "protect" me. My brother (after serving in Viet Nam) was married for a short time, had a beautiful baby daughter and then divorced. I recall him renting a house from my parents and unexpected drop-ins to "inspect the place" would thrust us into the belly of a beer blast or some other type of wild party. He never seemed settled or okay with who he was… always looking for something; almost troubled. When I was a very young child, one of my mother's "check-in" inspections, resulted in my running ahead of her into the house… seeing people laying everywhere, bottles strewn about and this strange large bowl filled with pretty colored "candies". As I reached my hand into the bowl to take some, a young woman grabbed my hand and sharply admonished, "No!" She squeezed my hand so tightly that I dropped the "candies" and ran into my brother's bedroom. I saw him sleeping along with two partially clad young women. I jumped into bed and yelled for him to wake up. He grabbed me, shushed me in a slurred sort of way and began to touch me in strange places. I was confused but he is my brother so my trust was complete. My mother walked through the bedroom threshold and began screaming at my brother. Bodies scampered and scattered like cockroaches in the light.

My mother grabbed me up, left the house and put me in the car. After she re-entered the house, the screaming continued until we left. She directed me to not tell Daddy what I saw or what he did. She said that Daddy would kill him... so I kept quiet. After all, there wasn't another thing needed or desired by me more than the love, acceptance and approval of my mother and I loved my brother and didn't want to see him dead.

Throughout adulthood, I thought my mother told my sister but to this day, I am unsure of that . If she knew, nothing was ever said and my brother never spoke of it but his pattern will re-emerge later in life. I deeply loved my brother and sister; still do. My father didn't know until I told him a couple of years ago... his reply... "Mama was right, I would've killed him." Secrets kept are a cancer to those keeping them. It was this same time of life that my parents made significant changes in our lives which would further change the course for each of us.

CHAPTER 2

When I was five Mother and Dad purchased a nursing home, which was right next to a nursing home that my grandparents owned and operated. The intention was to help others while making a nice living, which would in turn help my father retire from many years of factory work. We literally moved our residence into the nursing home and began to live amongst the elderly residents. At first I loved it. I had grandparents in them... interesting stories of exotic places and people... freely given wisdom... affection... a flow of visitors coming to see their loved ones, but things began to quickly erode.

My parents were busy 24/7, always away running errands for the residents and I began to feel the loss. My parents began to detach from me and became indifferent. I was a smart child who was able to instinctively sense what I was feeling and able to verbally communicate those feelings to others, but it got me nowhere. My pleas for more family time and attention fell on deaf ears. I remember wondering why they weren't listening to me... not hearing me.

As business picked up, I found myself feeling very angry, mostly at my parents but also at the elderly residents. They were more important to my parents than I was now... so I began to act out. I began to steal their false teeth in the middle of the night and switch them with other residents... or hide them all over the house, including in the toilet tank. I would put the men's underwear in the women's dresser drawers and short sheet their beds... hide their eyeglasses underneath potted plants and so much more. I would crawl behind the sofa and gently tug on their hair to confuse them, whispering hateful things in their ears as they were watching television and stealing the remote to change the channel during their polka program.

Since most of them were Alzheimer's patients, nobody caught on for quite some time, until I pulled a trick on a new resident who was there for other reasons. It took her all of two minutes to hate me and the war was ON! My clever skills expanded, as her accuracy in aiming for me with her cane improved! The battle raged on for what seemed like forever until her son met with my parents. I was immediately confronted and I stood in shock. How could anyone accuse me of such horrific things? I'm a good girl. Yeah, I was good; *real* good. Things still changed.

My parents hired a cook (my Nanny) who very rapidly became my confidant and friend. She was an interesting woman who had a keen vision for seeing the bigger picture and a willingness to call things as she saw them. She was a bright spot in my life; playing games, cooking together, laughing, telling jokes about the residents and yes it soothed my spirit.

I was no longer allowed to use the bedroom on the top floor. My bedroom was moved to the basement… a stone, cold, damp, unfinished basement without a toilet and lights that were too high to reach. Each night, the door leading in and out of the basement would be locked, from the inside of the upstairs; I can still hear the clicking of the old skeleton key as it secured my only way out. I was told that this had to be done so that I couldn't wreak havoc during the night, and since the door to the basement was right next to the door to the bathroom, they were protecting the residents from falling down the stairs. To me, I was locked in with no way out, no toilet to use, no lights, and no heat. I had a bed, metal wardrobes for clothes, a small round avocado green shag rug, a cedar hope chest, a blanket that never seemed to be enough to take the chill out of my bones and a drain in the floor in case I couldn't hold it until morning.

This went on for years but there was a bright spot each night. I recall lying in the damp, cold sheets of that bed and praying that God would be with me and keep me safe. Just like clockwork, as soon as daylight lifted the darkness of night, a time that I was most frightened and feeling alone, small lights would pass by the high basement windows on the ceiling line of the room. I would find myself warm, safe, peaceful and verbally thanking God for sending His precious angels to check on me. I was sure that they were angels and I no longer felt cold, achy or alone; for God was with me. I told my nanny about them and she just smiled and validated that God loved me. I thought she was hired to cook and to watch over me but a few years ago, my father told me that she was just the cook; not my nanny. Thank you, Daddy for sharing that with me, as it makes the memories even sweeter. You see, she gave to me, from a place of choice, not for a paycheck. Anna, you were really the Angel from God... thank you for being so kind and loving to me, walking the walk.

She has passed on by now but I always remembered the Bible verse she used to quote to me as she held me in her arms. Matthew 19:14... "But Jesus said, 'Suffer little children, and forbid them not, to come unto me; for of such is the kingdom of heaven.'"

It wasn't until many years later that I realized what was really coming through the windows at night; the headlights of passing cars.

CHAPTER 3

Within days of acquiring my new living quarters, other things changed… and further altered the course of my life. We weren't close to my grandparents and I didn't understand why, until we were immediately thrust into a daily interaction by living next door, which changed everything… forever!

The extreme religious legalistic limitations were in full force and the spiritual abuse began. My grandfather was a religious leader in the community for many years. My first memory of him was hearing him preach about fire and brimstone, while beating his Bible on the pulpit or the palm of his hand. Then he would extend that same hand to shake hands with those leaving the church, while his other hand was up my dress, as he had me in his arms. Didn't anybody notice or were they just star struck or fearful of the "man of God?" Either way, I believe my mother knew something, because I remember her grabbing me from his arms and we didn't go back to church for a long while. Now, we lived next door to them and although my parents had somewhat broken away from the strong religious legalism, he quickly stepped in to be the strong hand I "needed".

The beatings from my father had turned to indifference, I was locked nightly into the basement and in attempts to "get me out of her hair," Mother would send me to my grandparents' house daily. I would help with whatever they needed, unloading groceries, dishes, setting tables for dinner, bathing the old people or cleaning my grandparents' apartment in the basement of the old Victorian home. The basement had small rooms that were cold, damp and dimly lit. In a strange way, I felt comfortable here.

Wednesday mornings were Bible study with the elderly residents from their home. It was then that Grandpa would teach, preach and demand the full attention and respect from every resident in the house, a mandatory event. This was his stage and he was the star! I was forced to sit on his lap as he preached and passed the Bible around for each resident to read a verse. He would take out his little black leather coin purse; I immediately knew what that meant. If I didn't make a peep during this time, no matter *what* happened, then he would give me a shiny new penny from his pouch. If I tried to get down and leave, he would grab my little arms so hard that there would be finger bruises from his grasp. The Bible passing slowly and I wished they would read faster. He would reach up underneath my dress and take a tiny piece of tender flesh, from my inner thigh, between his fingernails and pinch… twist and *pull*, until the flesh popped back to my leg. If I didn't make a sound, then he moved to the inside of my underarm and repeated the process, trying to make me falter. The pain was sharp and my eyes stung with tears... but not a whisper from me. Not because I wanted the God-blessed shiny penny but because I didn't want to be dragged to the basement apartment for hours of prayer while on my knees. My mother saw the tiny bruises all over my underarms and inner thighs and when she inquired, I told her the truth, but she didn't believe me. Nothing changed.

The days turned to weeks and weeks to months. By this time, the money was flowing for my parents and weekend getaways were planned, but for me a bigger nightmare began. I was sent to stay with my grandparents for the weekend. Hours upon hours of kneeling and praying... my grandparents taking me into a closet underneath an old staircase and moving clothing aside to reveal a cross, mirror and a handle with leather straps hanging from it. Purging your sins they would call it. My grandmother sleeping upstairs because she would be up half of the night with the residents, so my grandfather would sleep with me in the downstairs apartment. The first time he took my hand, I was clueless, innocent and trusting. The veil of innocence was lifted from that day forward. He said, "Do this because I am a man of God and if you don't, God will send you to hell." He spoke of keeping bloodlines pure and how my mother was a harlot... a jezebel and he didn't want me to turn out like her. I heard all about hell in his sermons, so I was scared not to do as this man of God was instructing me. When my mother returned, I told her what happened and she refused to believe me, telling me to keep my mouth shut or it could cause them to lose their business and Daddy would have to return to the factory. So, in hopes of keeping or getting in my mother's good graces, I didn't make a whisper...but the price paid was great. Not only did I pay the price but so did others. My acting out became focused not only toward the elderly people in my grandmother's Home but also towards my grandparents in general.

I began to do things like steal my grandfather's keys and bury them in the garden, staple the flap of his underwear shut, stock the canned goods in the wrong rooms, hide frozen fish in strategic places and watch with eagerness as they rotted. I started the same antics with the elderly as before, but this time added new tricks to my skill set. I started stealing their canes, eye glasses, false teeth and purses; burying them in the garden. I moved clothing between closets, stole all of the toilet paper out of bathrooms and moved family pictures around from room to room. When asked to paint their kitchenette in the basement apartment, I urinated in the paint (wringing my hands in a mischievous manner)! They deeply complained for days about the rank smell in their kitchen. No, I'm not proud of the things I did as a child but nobody was hearing my verbal cries for help, so I thought maybe they'd hear me now. It's interesting what a strong will and healthy mind can create in order to survive.

After three – four years of this, weekends away became frequent and I felt his instructions and demands were becoming more brazen. He began telling me about the difference between boys and girls and what certain body parts do; things were beginning to progress to a new level and somehow I instinctually knew this... I also knew something had to change.

One day, I was being forced to take one of his afternoon naps with him. While he was asleep, I began to slowly and carefully slither out of the bed and quietly creep out of the apartment. I went to a large warehouse in the rear of our properties and hid inside. After many hours of hearing people yelling for me, my mother came in, scoured the building and found me. After slapping me in the face over and over, for ignoring her calls, she asked me why I was hiding. I told her everything and World War Three unfolded. Why hadn't she believed me all of these years? Why didn't she protect me? If only my pleas from the beginning would have been heard and action taken... only speculation that renders little or no comfort at this point.

In my eighth year of life, my grandfather died and I was set free of his spiritual, sexual and physical abuse. My mother forced me to kiss his cheek, as he lay in the casket and the cold hardness of his skin caused me to vomit. As some of his belongings were divvied up, I asked for the little black leather coin pouch, filled with shiny new pennies. I have it to this day as a reminder to NEVER let anyone in my life use the name of God for their personal pleasure.

After many years of physical, emotional, verbal and sexual abuse I began to see God moving in my life in strange ways. I had started a new Christian Private School and the pastor's wife Betty was beautiful. A loving, integrity-filled, gentle woman that played a personal motherly role in my life, giving me the genuine Godly influence, that I so desperately needed. She began to work with me on my singing voice which later took me to classical performance and working as a vocal coach in New York City, for a short period of time.

CHAPTER 4

Shortly after my grandfather passed, life in my basement bedroom changed. I was sleeping one night in February and it was storming outside. The lightning and thunder woke me and the smell in the basement was staggering. I swung my legs over the side of the bed and they landed in knee deep freezing water. I am so cold and now so wet. What's going on? It's so dark and I can't find the chair, and I can't reach the light bulb in the ceiling without it. I make my way to the cedar hope chest and resting atop, is a junior baton given to me by a school friend. I'm so scared and begin screaming for help. I climb on top of the chest and using the baton, begin to beat on the ceiling for what feels like hours. I know my parents and most residents sleep two floors up but somebody has to hear me. Why can't they hear me? Please, God, help me.

The frantic beating on the ceiling turns to a methodical tapping. The screams turn to silence… and the backed up sewer water gets deeper. Will I die here? Trapped in this basement alone? I've been buried for a long time now anyway... Doesn't anybody care? Am I not important to anybody? God, please help me!

Moments later, I hear bustling from upstairs and running through the upstairs floor. I hear the sweet familiar sound of the skeleton key hitting the keyhole and turning, as it unlocks the door. I cannot move... I cannot speak... I hear my brother's voice calling out for me and I cannot speak. The lights go on and the bulb that's just inches from my face blinds me. So close to the bulb but fear kept me from looking for it. My brother is yelling something to my mother about sewage backups all over town, but I cannot make out what else he's saying; it sounds foreign to me. I feel my eyes slightly shift to look around me; only to see everything covered in sludge... ruined... filthy... *including me*! My brother waded through the basement, swept me up in his arms and carried me out of the basement for the last time in my life... saving my life! I was worth saving!

From that night forward, my bedroom was on the third floor and although I was safe and not locked away each night. I was forever changed! I went from a little girl to a little adult, overnight. I began to cook three meals a day on my nanny's days off and gave baths to the old people in three homes, males alike. Although nothing sexual ever took place from the time my grandfather died, a child giving baths to elderly adults would be considered abusive in its own right; my mother paid me well.

I learned at an early age that money was evil, work is more important than family, self-sacrifice is worth acceptance or approval, crying out for help doesn't do any good, silence kept... keeps you safe and if all else fails; vengeance. These messages played out in my daily life for many years to come and affected every relationship I have ever had, until this point.

I packed my hard-earned money away into my new bank account, cleaned up the cedar hope chest and began to pack things for my future; things that gave me hope of being free from the bondage I had lived.

After a year filled with many residents, who I had grown to love... passing away... the emotional loss took a toll on me. Finding residents cold and stiff in their beds, one that was young and became my best friend... took her own life during the night and others that would be ushered off to the hospital and never return. It was all too much to bear for anyone, let alone a young ten year old. During a conversation with my mother, she told me, "You have to stop loving these people because they are all dying off." Oh my God, my love is killing them. I can't love them or they'll die... another message that I carried until I was in my mid-thirties. I now know what she meant by that piece of advice, but at the time, I was only ten or eleven with limited emotional understanding. As if emotions were a water spigot, I immediately turned off love and turned on the cold, professional, detached, matter-of-factness that I carried with me through my college years; yet each Friday I ritualistically walked downtown and purchased a single red rose for my mother. Could I ever do enough or be enough to win her love, affection, approval and acceptance? When I was twelve years old, my parents moved us to another home, separate from the nursing home, which started a new chapter of my life. This was the end of the beginning.

PART 2

The Lost Walk

CHAPTER 5

Our new home created the separateness I needed to regain a sense of family and enter a new time of life with some sense of normalcy. I continued growing throughout high school, all the while diligently seeking to please and gain the approval and acceptance of my Mom. My hopes were high that we could have more as a family and the bond could be reconnected in a healthy manner, but this wasn't to be. My parents found themselves having to travel across town to resolve issues and something always came up. I no longer blamed the elderly residents; I blamed my parents... they were allowing all of this to happen and the patterns, messages and pathology was set in place.

With optimistic hopes for change and an undying compulsion to see "happiness" within our family, I would excessively clean the house, having very little social life; being the "goody two shoes" as my sister used to call me. Nothing seemed to work; the best achieved was indifference. She was financially driven, status driven, politically driven and certainly close to my sister but not much of who I was or what I achieved got her attention, so I stopped trying. I felt angry and when I tried to talk to her about it, she brushed me off, literally pushed my shoulder and walk past me and out of the room. She didn't want to hear it. She didn't want to hear anything that would be a distraction from her making money or spending it; messages galore. I'm not important enough to even listen to, my feelings are insignificant, I'm a bother, I'm not wanted, loved; I'm nothing to her and money is evil.

Money? I had grown to hate money and my anger went unnoticed by her, so on an impulse, I acted out. She used to leave her purse wide open with hundreds of dollars just wadded up or laying loose in her open purse. I decided impulsively to hit her where I felt she would feel it… her money! So, I reached my twelve year old fingertips into the purse and grabbed two one hundred dollar bills, stuffed them into my pocket and left. For days I kept waiting for the explosives to detonate but nothing happened. Day after day, week after week, month after month, not a word said; no confrontations, not even a conversation overheard of missed money. She has so much money she didn't even notice two hundred dollars was missing? And yet she was putting the art of making money over everyone and everything else in her life? Money is evil and causes people to get sucked into a frame of mind where nothing else matters! Don't get sucked in, "don't have money," a message I still struggle with to this day.

Being a good girl or a "goody two shoes" as my sister called me, I found this act of betrayal and theft, haunting every minute of every day for over two and a half years. Guilt that was so devastating to me but I knew that I had no choice but to make it right. So, by the time I was ready to make it right, I was fourteen and a half years old and had taken a waitress job. Before working my first shift ever, I approached my mother and asked her to sit down and please listen to me. She did and I opened my heart and told her what I had done wrong over two years prior and why I had done it! I cried, I asked for forgiveness and I told her I had gotten a job, that I was starting that very day and that I would be paying her back double plus interest of her choice. I knew this was going to make me vulnerable and ran the risk of losing all chances of gaining the love, affection, acceptance and approval that I had so longed and worked for my whole life. However, if I was going to be okay with me, I had to do it and do it right. I thought for sure she would at least forgive me for making my first truly big mistake and would respect me for my forthcoming honesty, let alone my willingness to make it right financially including her choice of interest. After all, money talked with Mom. I didn't have a clue what to really expect, other than I thought she would of course "tell Daddy when he got home"... sigh. I knew I'd have to deal with that. Her reaction took my breath away. She became irate with me, telling me that she would never trust me again in my life, that I was a mere thief, a loser of sorts, a common criminal. She informed that she was taking my house key away, telling everyone in our family that I cannot be trusted in their homes or around their purses. Then she proceeded to tell me that the interest she was charging me was 100% interest per year compounding. By the time I finished paying her off, the total paid was $800 cash and it took me a month of tips and paychecks to do it. All those years of not protecting me but bless her heart, she sure protected our family from me though.

For the rest of her life she announced at every family get together or event, for everyone not to leave their purses lying about because Mitzey is a thief and she'll steal from you! She never trusted me again, never showed any level of respect for my eventual honesty and making restitution; instead she seized the opportunity to humiliate, degrade, undermine any trust or respect from others. Further she stuck those horrible messages down my throat to the point where at times I could not breathe or even catch my breath. She had turned my family against me and even family friends had lost trust and respect in me. I kept silent. I didn't protect myself, defend myself or run away. I just lowered my head and took it because that's what I was taught to do, I felt I had deserved it, but this was getting old! Something had to change and I was going to change it! I started by not attending as many events, where this process could be repeated. In a sense, I was starting to be pushed out of the family cortex; was that a bad thing? Pondering.

CHAPTER 6

I began to do for me, think for myself, meet my own needs, begin a few friendships, started to date a nice young man with good values and a nice family, as well as work my job. Things were looking up and all the while finding solace within my vocal performances. I loved to express myself through song, thanks to the same pastor's wife from my church school. I had grown a little closer to my sister and her family; even my brother would make his presence known at family functions and such that I did attend. Overall, life had improved greatly and I was grateful; why? Not because they were changing but because I was changing!

Shortly before graduating high school, I was bitten by a brown-recluse spider and overnight became very ill. It was my brother who called the house, heard my voice and being a paramedic, recognized that something was seriously wrong with me. He contacted emergency services and a short time later, I was pulled from the bathtub that I was soaking in and once again my brother saved my life. I had gone into anaphylactic shock, was rushed to the hospital where they frantically worked to keep me alive. I will never forget gaining consciousness and seeing my mother standing in the room crying. I was shocked to see any emotion from her. I looked down toward my feet, as I felt someone with their hand on my foot. I couldn't see anybody there, but I felt the sweetest peace I have ever known during that moment. I heard an audible voice tell me, "You're dying but it's okay; you're not alone, you've never been alone." I felt total and utter peace that passes all understanding. No pain, no sorrow, no regret, just peace and love. I blinked my eyes thinking I would then see who was touching my foot but upon opening my eyes, there wasn't anyone there. I knew who it was. I had already met Him many years before, in the cold, dark, damp, wet basement. I opened my eyes and my mother approached the gurney. I told her that I was dying and it was okay; "Don't be sad, Mama, don't cry, Jesus is here with me."

It was at that moment that I heard a doctor say, "We're losing her," and that was that. I awoke quite some days later very ill but alive. The nurses told me that my heart had stopped twice before they could stabilize me, and that I had been unconscious for many days. Recovery took over a year but I will never forget the words said to me that day and the feeling of peace, that I was given. That message of love, peace and not being alone has followed me throughout adulthood and will until the day that I hold His hand and walk streets of gold with Him.

That next year was filled with recovery and a newfound urgency from my mother; some level of influence over my life. Although their hearts were in the right place and I knew it at the time, they attempted to do so by controlling my thoughts, choices and feelings. Wait a minute, indifference, career-driven, blinded by money and financial stability, my whole childhood! I almost die and now you choose to show you care by putting the clamps on me? I lovingly played along, because I still wanted to win the love, affection, attention, approval and acceptance of my mother but underlying issues remained and affected our daily relationship. During that year, I graduated from high school and was accepted to a college. I was going to be the first person in the history of my family (on both sides) to ever go to a four year college and that, I thought, was my sure ticket in achieving the ultimate; Mom's approval. That year brought about other events that were sure to change the course of history in our family.

CHAPTER 7

I have always held a special place in my heart for my brother's daughter. She was a sweet little long-haired blonde with big eyes and a precious disposition. She was ten or eleven years younger than I, but I grew older hearing stories of my brother not being there for her emotionally and her feeling lonely and sad. This always tugged at my heartstrings, so I took it upon myself to reach out to her and try to spend time nurturing her. I could see my young self in her and I needed to be a bright spot for her, as others had been for me.

When I overheard my parents talking about my brother being accused of fondling her, I was overwrought with emotion. I approached my mother, while my father was out of the house and the conversations began. Many heated conversations about the fact that she didn't come forth when I was little, that she didn't protect me, didn't hold him accountable and that because of that, he's done it to his own daughter and it's sure to happen again. I knew this; not because I was a child expert in the field but because I somehow knew and I guess, in a way, I was an expert. It was sometime during one of these conversations that my future path was crystallized; I was to advocate for those sexually exploited. I became adamant that my mother report him... hold him accountable and make this right! She refused and became viciously angry with me. Realizing that I wasn't getting anywhere with her and my emotions were too high, I left the house to cool down. I walked to my sister's house.

I attempted to approach her on the issue and it quickly turned to her protecting our brother, making excuses and demanding that I keep my mouth shut. The same messages sent and received by her, as well as my mother. My efforts were futile, so the conversation ended.

I felt that I needed to be responsible in my own right, so I went to the police station and asked to speak to an officer, who was standing by his cruiser, outside the station. I explained the situation and how my brother touched me as a child and now his own daughter has accused him of the same. He asked what my brother's name was, as he was taking notes on a little pad of paper. When I said his name, immediately his face changed and he lifted his head and just looked at me. He mentioned that my brother was highly revered locally, and I was promptly told that there wasn't anything he could do; that I should go home and forget about it. Why was everyone trying to sweep this under the rug? I couldn't trust my family or even the police to make this right! Little did my family know, at that time, that my brother would go on to commit adultery and be accused of fondling his step-daughter. Family secrets continued to be covered up and I knew it would eventually happen again.

Many arguments ensued, between my mother and me, over this issue and of course she lured my father into the equation, by inciting his anger, but nothing prepared me for what was to come.

I frustratingly returned home and tried to reason with my mother, again. She argued that my brother had worked so hard to get his life straightened out, create a locally high profile career and that he would lose that, plus everything he knew and loved. Where was the love when he inappropriately touched me, showed me girlie magazines when I was younger and now touching his daughter? When she began to bring up what people would think of our family, is when I lost it. Years of pent up emotion, resentment and hurt emerged and I began to scream at her, throw things and telling her that she was being a "bitch". "I cannot be a part of this evil any longer," I said.

"Then get out," she said.

At that moment, my father entered the house and of course, she turned on the tears, telling him details of things that I said. But she left out what she had said, so I merely left the room so as to not enrage my father; after all, I remembered what that was like. As I was walking up the spiral staircase to my room, I heard her tell him, "…and she called me a bitch." Here it comes… that's going to really make Daddy mad.

CHAPTER 8

I began to undress for bed and got down to my bra and half slip, only to hear my father stomp up the staircase. I yelled at him, making sure he knew that I was half nude, but that meant nothing to him; he was in a rage. He entered my room and the second I saw the look on his face, I knew it was going to get bad. He didn't say a word, as he began to beat me with his fists, while pinning me to the floor. He began to rip out handfuls of hair, wrapping his hands around my long hair and slamming my head against the open-brick chimney, which ran through my bedroom. He said, "I'm going to kill you" and never seeing this look on his face before, I believed him. Blood began to fly through the air, hitting walls, carpet, brick chimney and even the steeply sloped ceiling. I was begging him to stop. "Daddy, please stop. I'm sorry, Daddy, I won't ever say that again to Mama!" but the punches to my face continued, as handfuls of hair were being ripped from my scalp. I felt my rage begin to boil and years full of anger, resentment, hurt and never defending myself, took over.

I began to scream mean things to him, punching him back in the face, until I was weak with exhaustion; his strength and rhythm never wavered. My mother was now behind him. I could see her face and her attempts to pull him off of me. I said, "Mama, please stop, Daddy, don't let him kill me!", but nothing from her. The harder I fought, the more aggressive he became. This seemed to go on for what felt like an hour and I began to beg and cry again, until my body went limp. The pain was unbearable, but he just kept punching. I guess Mother got him to stop and go downstairs, because when my eyes opened, I could hear them yelling. As I got my bearings, I can still recall the feeling of the carpet texture, beneath my fingertips, as I gently stroked it; just to make sure I was still alive. I knew I had to save myself, but I was so weak and there was so much blood everywhere. The pain was horrible and my eyes were nearly swollen shut and burning so badly; I think from the blood in them.

It was winter outside but I decided to quietly, and as quickly as I could, drag myself down the staircase and sneak out the front door that wasn't used much. For a second, it reminded me of slithering out of my grandfather's bed while he was sleeping. I had on a half slip and a bra, which were both covered in blood. No shoes, no coat, no pants, but I began to walk... somewhere safe, but where? "Hurry Mitzey, before they see that I'm gone and come looking for me," I said to myself. The freezing snow crunched beneath my feet; with each kneed deep step, I left a trail of blood. I was barely walking when I got to a friend's house, climbed up the stairs of their front porch, knocked on the door and then I heard, "Oh my God what happened…?"

I must have passed out, because the next thing I knew I was at the hospital and being treated. Everyone had thought I had been raped because I was unable to speak and so brutally beaten. I refused to be examined, as I was a virgin and knew that I had not been raped. I adamantly refused with the flailing of my arms, as that would have been a violation to me. My friend's parents called my boyfriend, who promptly came to the hospital with his family and stayed by my side. Through their own anger and sadness for me, they were able to give wise counsel and asked me to stay with their family, until I was strong enough and could figure out my next step. The police did nothing because I didn't have proof that it was my father who beat me. By this time, the police were good for nothing in my mind.

After two weeks of recovery, I snuck into my parents' house, took fifty dollars I had saved up and hid in my dresser drawer, a sleeping bag, pillow and my ten-speed bike. My bank deposit book was gone from my drawers. I knew she had taken it, but I was too scared to confront her and I had to get out of the house fast! The bank informed me that because I was a minor, they could not release the funds to me without parental consent. They called my mother who demanded that no monies be released to me, even though it was my money, and that the bank was to keep me from leaving their premises. I ran out and never returned to my parents' home to live; instead, I cut contact and went to my first semester of college.

CHAPTER 9

When my parents had heard that I followed through with going to my first semester of college and it was on their dime, my mother attempted to contact me; which I carefully avoided at all cost. She left messages with my room-mate, stating that I would not be able to return to college the next semester if I didn't talk to them. I called and agreed to meet my mother for a cup of coffee but refused to be in my father's presence. For God's sake, I still had patches of hair missing from my scalp and she wanted me to make amends with him? I was done. I tried to obtain financial aid, but due to holding dependent status, my hands were tied. Alternative decisions had to be made, but what were my options. My boyfriend's family had become my own and they continued to give wise counsel and lovingly show me approval and acceptance, but my time at this college would soon be up. Between the financial issues of attending a Bible College and that college dropping my desired degree, I began to apply to other State Universities.

A college in the Chicago area accepted my application. I wasn't able to get assistance but my mother agreed to pay for one semester at the university, with strings attached... many strings. I paid the price of being controlled and started the new university with her money. My boyfriend's mother told me that I should just use her money; after all, didn't I earn that money when I was a child. The years of sacrifice, emotional abuse and the fact that every ounce of the sexual abuse I had endured was on her hands, as much as those that perpetrated the crimes? My attitude was 'use her'. This new, angry attitude wasn't attractive and the relationship with my boyfriend of three years began to disintegrate. I was mortified... not just because he was the first guy that ever showed interest, treated me with love and respect but also because his family was the only family I had ever really known. That was a good example of what family should be. They had become my family too and now I was losing everything. I began to unravel in my thinking. I became clingy and needy, which of course caused the relationship to end even sooner. I was done with everyone and everything!

I cut ties with everyone in my life, walked out of my college dorm and went to stay with a new friend I had met from downtown Chicago, just for a weekend. She was a nice girl but was pressuring me to "make up with my parents". My friend had spoken to my mother over the phone and was lovingly persuasive. Mother could be so friendly to others; to a point where people were taken in by her generosity and charm. Not me, at that time, I saw her as a cold, detached, emotionally unavailable, manipulative user of others that was too self-consumed to protect her own child from harm. However, when she was nice to me, I bought into it and thought that this was a sign of things changing; only to be devastated when the truth surfaced. So, with the same fifty dollars I had saved from home, my ten-speed bike, sleeping bag and the clothes on my back, I left her apartment and disappeared! My car was left at the university, my room, belongings I had accumulated over a short six months and everyone who had ever hurt me. I just disappeared.

Where would I go? Where would I sleep? How would I eat? All valid questions that I didn't have answers for but I knew I was free and safer in the parks of Chicago than in my own family.

The first night I slept in a public bathroom; locking the door behind me I vacillated all night between crying and feeling peaceful. The next day, I got a waitress job at a little diner and committed to two shifts per day, five days per week. I found that I could shower at the YWCA for a few dollars of tip money and the diner fed me during both shifts. Wow, I had it made; freedom from control, abuse, use and misuse. It was proving to be safer on the streets of Chicago, than it was in my own home. What would I eat on my two days off? I heard about Pacific Garden Mission – an inner-city ministry helping those in need. They fed the homeless, held church services and were an overall outreach. I didn't need their help; I was free and better than I had been in years. This was something that I could donate my time to on my days off so I did and they in turn, fed me in all ways possible. Thank you, God, for once again sending more of your angels in my direction.

Days turned to weeks, which quickly turned to months, but I was never harmed in any way, nor did I ever turn to substances, illegal activity or exploiting myself. Amazing I know, but it's true. I saw many things during this time of my life, yet I seemed to be under this dome of protection that I had never felt before. I had seen muggings in the park, homeless people that froze to death while sleeping on park benches, a rape and even a stabbing at one point. Even though I had never been homeless before, I had learned the art of hiding and avoiding danger at a young age! And again, something was protecting me. Instead of using my childhood experiences as an excuse to do wrong, I chose to become what God intended me to be all along... a strong, loving and giving young woman of integrity.

After seeing a woman beaten and raped in the park, I was deeply moved. I began working part-time at a rape crisis center during the night shift, which kept me dry, warm and safe. The missionaries didn't know that I was homeless, until one of the visitors recognized me. They told the leader, who in turn sat down and had a loving, wise conversation with me; once again changing the course of my life forever.

After a period of time, many great things began to happen in my life and doors opened that I never thought were possible. I went to the East Coast, vocally performing and a vocal coach, taking college courses (thanks to financial aid and gaining independent status), traveling throughout Europe backpacking and vocally performing for churches on a rotation. Love offerings were given and although that didn't make me wealthy, I was giving back and doing what made me happy. The contacts and friends I had made at Pacific Gardens changed my life. I wanted to be an angel of light that brightened the nights of others; even if it was through song. Life was good and so was I! My walk in life had gone from lost… to found! (was I ever lost?)

CHAPTER 10

Life continued on this peaceful, joy-filled path, while living on the East Coast. I was kind to everyone and began to trust everyone without question. Every morning I had a cup of coffee at a local diner that serviced business people and dock workers alike. I always thought it funny because you could walk into the diner any morning and see the bar filled with suits and fishing slickers. They were all walking different paths in life, but one thing brought them together each morning, coffee! I was kind to everyone, hoping to be a bright spot in their day maybe even uplifting to their spirits. My life seemed to be peaceful and full, and yet there was this sad place of longing for a loving family. Longing for what could have been, what should have been, what might be, hope remained; until a man misinterpreted my friendliness.

One of the fishermen who I had met in the diner, came by my apartment. Yes, he had been there before, when I had a little get-together with others, but we had only had a couple of one-on-one conversations at the diner; nothing that was romantic in nature and certainly nothing that was flirtatious. He knocked on the door and when I looked through the peephole, it was Brett. "What are you doing here, Brett?" He mumbled something which I couldn't hear. "What did you say?" I asked. He repeated it but I couldn't understand what he was saying so I made a very critical mistake that changed my life. I opened the door so I could hear him; a nearly fatal mistake. He pushed in the door, knocking me to the floor. I was so shocked, I didn't even scream. "Brett, what are you doing? What's wrong with you?" I cried. His speech was incoherent and obviously something was wrong, or not right with him; he was different than I'd ever seen him before. He was erratic, sweating profusely and rambling on incoherently. After slamming the door, he began to slap me across my face. I started screaming and fighting back but just like my father, the harder I fought, the meaner he became. He ripped my nightgown with one hand, as the other hand pulled out a filet knife, which normally rested in a leather pouch on his belt. Holding that knife to my throat he began to touch me with his other hand. His body was heavily weighing me down, to keep me still. I begged him, "Please Brett, we are friends. Don't hurt me, I've always been kind to you and I'm your friend. Please, Brett, I'm only nineteen and a virgin. I'm saving myself for my husband, please, Jesus loves you Brett and so do I"… and with that last word, he took the knife and sliced around my right nipple. I screamed out in agony, but he put the knife back to my throat and told me that he would kill me if I "made a peep."

I'd heard that before... but where? "Don't make a peep"...... that's right... "Don't make a peep and I'll give you a shiny new penny"...... Dammit; not again... not this! I began to fight for my life, kneeing him in the groin, biting anything I could get in my mouth, but even though I was able to break free, I wasn't able to reach the door. I kept screaming for help but nobody came. As I was running for the door, he hit me on the back of the head with the butt of the knife and I fell to the floor and passed out. I do recall my body feeling like a rag doll as I hit the hardwood floor and yet the fall seemed to be in slow motion. I came to, while he was raping me. My breasts hurt so badly and there was blood everywhere. I was numb, in shock, brutally beaten and didn't have the energy to fight any longer. I lay there, with my head turned to the side and quietly wept through my beaten and swollen shut eyes. As he finished, he took the filet knife and cut my inner thighs and inside of my vagina. I felt this agonizing pain shooting through my body and am now reliving the pain, by merely typing these words.

Brett ran from the apartment but told me that if I said anything about this to anyone, he would come back and finish the job. I just lay there, unable to move or make a sound. I wanted to die. "Please God, just let me die and come to you," but there were other plans. A neighbor soon thereafter returned home from work, saw my door open and ran to go call for help. I remember the doctor from the free clinic down the street, rushing up to see if he could help. His kind words, gentle touch on my forehead and whispers of God in my ear kept me alive. I wish I could recall his name but I feel time, and my mind, have caused certain aspects to be blocked out. Brett was never found and I refused to be of any help in prosecuting him, even if they did. I should have never opened the door and that action caused me to feel responsible. I had a victim mentality. I must have deserved it; did something wrong.

After my hospital stay and reconstructive surgeries were over, I stayed with a friend until I could gain strength, figure out what to do and where to go next. I had no family to call and very few true friends. I was petrified to return to my apartment so I never did; once again leaving everything behind. Two friends went and packed up suitcases with most of my prized possessions but the rest was left where it set. I had gotten good at leaving everyone and everything behind. I wasn't worth protecting and standing up for. I was responsible, who would believe me? Who cares anyway?

I had heard years later that Brett was arrested and convicted of another rape and attempted murder, which occurred prior to mine. Brick walls to no walls that didn't work either! Now what? More brick walls? Messages, patterns and pathology continue. Different faces but threads of the same themes followed.

CHAPTER 11

While I was staying with a friend for a few weeks recuperating, I got a call from an old friend from my hometown. She told me that she heard my mother was very ill, but unable to be diagnosed. Something about chest pains and that she had been going to specialists to figure it out. I found myself being heavily harassed once again. I hesitantly picked up the phone and called my mother, after all of this time and inquired on her health. She began to cry and ask about me. I tearfully told her that I had gone through a terrible assault and almost didn't make it through it. She wanted to know the details of what had happened to me but I wasn't ready or willing to share it with anyone; let alone her. We both cried and she said she would call me back in ten minutes. Five minutes later she called and said that she and Daddy were packing the motor home and driving out to get me and bring me home. This was the last thing I wanted to do, but being so incredibly fearful of Brett's return to finish the job I agreed. I figured, if nothing else, it was a free ride to get far away from there. So, I started my return to Chicagoland once again.

The ride to Chicago was peaceful. My father and mother were kind and generous; in a way I had never seen before. They didn't ask any questions about my ordeal but just gave me gentle loving glances, without trails of criticism or judgment. What has happened? This was a new scene to me, unfamiliar unpredictable. It felt like I was on a vacation with them of some sort. They allowed me my space, accepted my silence, didn't inquire when I awoke screaming and handed me tissues when I quietly wept. These weren't my parents. I know that time apart and life experienced, during that separation had changed me could it possibly be that it had changed them too? Guard up, girl. The best predictor of future behavior is past patterns. I saw that my mother still kept her purse hidden, or with her, when I was around but I figured that aspect may never change; money has always been too important to her for that.

I transferred college transcripts and credits, got a waitress job, rented a little apartment from my parents and tried to settle down, all within 24 hours. Within two days of my return, my sister had a birthday party for someone and I was invited. I reluctantly agreed to attend for a short time, but was extremely anxious. I hadn't seen any of these people in quite some time now, nearly three years but I thought I would make an effort to show my face; mistake.

As I walked into the party, everyone turned and looked at me and gasped, followed by snickering and whispers. I heard words like, fat, her face is all bruised and swollen, she looks horrible and what has she done to herself. These were things I didn't need to hear, but I smiled and quickly moved through the crowd and through the doors, to the interior of the house. With windows open, I could clearly hear the gossip taking place outside, like maybe she got beat up by her pimp. Pimp? I was so numb that it just didn't matter to me. I said hello to those indoors and made my way through the house and exited the front door, to where my car was parked. I quickly left and went to my safe haven; my apartment.

The next day I had an appointment with a local gynecologist; the doctor that helped my mother bring me into the world. He was also the doctor who my sister worked for, as his nurse, but that didn't concern me. I was going to honestly share with the doctor; not his nurses. I would have gone to another doctor but this small town didn't have any others that I knew of. I told the doctor nothing but as he was giving me a check-up, he gasped and said, "What has happened to you, honey?" I swore him to confidentiality and asked that nothing be put in my file. He agreed so I proceeded to give him details. He sat in the chair and tears ran down his cheeks. He was a lovely man who I felt safe with and I knew could help me. I seemed to have had some kind of infection and the place where I was cut wasn't healing properly. It'd only been a month since it happened, but it bled daily and I was having real problems. My rectum had been cut too and the infection was coming from that issue. He gave me pills to take and well-defined instructions. He said he'd have to document the pills in the chart but nothing else; he would keep a private chart so my sister wouldn't have access. He understood that rape would "dishonor" my family, in their view and I might be treated differently. He kindly hugged me, told me he would be in contact and not to have any sexual contact with anyone. I assured him that wouldn't be a problem that I'd never had any sexual contact with anyone out of my choice! I left his office and returned to my waitress job, just down the street.

Within hours, my sister barged into the restaurant, during lunch rush hour, charged up to me and said, "You whore, you filthy f***ing whore... you've been having anal sex." I was beyond mortified, but was not going to tolerate this. I grabbed her by the arm, escorted her out of the restaurant and into a side hallway that led to the bathroom. I put my hands on her shoulders and pushed her up against the wall hard. I slapped her across her face as hard as I could and said, "You stupid bitch, I was raped! Why do you think my body is all swollen and still black and blue, even though it's been five weeks". I told her to never come to my place of work again and that what I told him was to be confidential. She said that the meds he prescribed me, were for women who have traces of bowel excrement in their vagina. Nice Sis... thanks! She proceeded to scream and yell at me about how she didn't believe me. I twirled around again and slapped her in the mouth, telling her that she was no longer a sister to me and hadn't been for many years! She just left with a shocked look on her face and this was never spoken of again.

CHAPTER 12

A year had passed. During this year, many events took place. I graduated with one degree and took classes towards another. I had moved into an apartment with another college student and within months, romantic feelings evolved. He was a nice guy and treated me with love, tenderness and respect. This was something I had not experienced for many years. I had never been sexually involved with anyone; still feeling worthless and unimportant since my virginity was taken from me at nineteen, things progressed quickly.

Within a year, we were engaged and at the same time I became very sick, yet nobody could seem to diagnose the problem. After seeing six different doctors and all of them telling me it was stress related, I ended up at the hospital Emergency Room. I had gained 80 pounds in three short months, was lactating, having erratic cycles, major mood swings, loss of vision plus I couldn't keep anything down. This hospital visit revealed a shocking discovery. I was diagnosed with a large benign brain and pituitary tumor, which was growing around and pinching my optic nerve. I was also determined to be three weeks pregnant. My new fiancé and I were in shock. The doctor told my family everything, without my consent, so the war started. I was horribly sick and yet their criticism, judgment, anger, name-calling and shaming began. I had dishonored my family by getting pregnant out of wedlock and that's all they focused on.

I transferred to a hospital in Chicago that specializes in these types of tumors and I was told that the tumor was large and required immediate surgery. There was only one problem they informed me that they would not do the surgery as long as I was with child. The tumor was growing so quickly and their medical opinions were that I would not survive nine months without surgery. Even if the baby were lucky enough to survive being born early, the child would more than like be severely disfigured and defective. They said they could schedule me for a medically necessary abortion and I was mortified at the thought of killing a baby; under any circumstances. This was against everything I believe in! I figured we're all defective anyway. Right? I wasn't about to play God. I figured, I have my fiancé and God will do His will, with all of this mess. The thought of a baby kind of excited me and petrified me all at the same time. So against doctor's advice, we returned home to let God's will be done.

My family didn't support us on any level. We were being slammed or shunned. Why? What were they hoping that would solve? Or was it a form of control? All I knew was that I loved God and wanted to do the right thing and with the support of my fiancé, anything was possible. Days passed, I got sicker and my vision became weaker. I was unable to work due to severe headaches and my fiancé decided that we needed to "rethink" getting married, so I gave the ring back. Within three weeks, he stopped making meals, stopped coming home to check on me throughout the day and started drinking beer. I'd never known him to drink but he wouldn't talk to me. All he said was that my family was really rough to him. I can only imagine!

CHAPTER 13

Within three weeks, the vision in my right eye was nearly gone. All I saw was flashes of lights and colors, nothing with structure. I got really scared and called the doctors. They informed me that the tumor was growing quickly and pinching the optic nerve more severely. They reminded me that eventually I would lose all sight until they were able to remove the tumor and lessen the pressure. This would require fetal termination. *No way!* So I waited, waited on God, waited for my fiancé to come back around and waited for my family to support me; at least giving me some wise words. Nothing! Complete shunning. I was a mar on their lives; once again, not worthy of even giving encouragement to. I drew closer to the Lord through prayer and my faith was strong even though I felt like I had let God down too.

Without warning, my fiancé packed his things and left, while I was sleeping one afternoon. A phone call from him later, explained that he just couldn't be saddled down with a sick wife and a baby too, so he needed to get some space. Space? Really? I lay in bed and just cried. I cried so hard that the pain in my head began to throb. This didn't stop for three days... unable to get myself any food, barely able to make my way to the bathroom and on the third day, I had a grand mal seizure. When it was over, I had very little vision from either eye and I was bruised all over from the severe thrashing that took place during the seizure. I tried calling people to help but nobody was there, no family, no friends, no fiancé, only the doctors.

I couldn't go on any longer! The doctors sent transportation for me and I was taken to a well-known University Hospital in Chicago, for surgery. I cried all of the way there because I knew that this meant that I would have to terminate my baby. I can still smell the leather from the inside of that car. I can still hear the sound of my quiet tears hitting the leather seats and the pain in my heart far exceeded the pain in my head. A decision was made but so were others.

I knew that ending a life is murder. I am thereby a murderer to many. You can't justify it because the life was living within my body versus walking amongst us! By this time in my life I had walked away from religion but I knew in my gut it was wrong to take a life, any life. I am choosing to share this for one reason only. *You have a choice* to make and I made mine but don't think that it has gone without consequences. Every single day of my life I think of that little girl (yes, I was told it was a girl, a deformed little girl) and every year on August 11, I silently celebrate my love for that unborn child. What could have been, what should have been, what needed to be, what could have I done differently. What could others have done differently? I have paid a price, so make your *choices* ladies but know that you too will have a price to pay; let alone the child, his or her price, their life, their life's possibilities, dreams, desires and so forth!

My heart was broken, as I lay in that hospital bed waiting for surgery. The three days prior to surgery, I had many grand mal seizures and totally lost my vision in both eyes. The doctors reassured me that some of that would return but to what extent they could not guarantee. I did have family that came to the hospital but what appeared to be supportive acts, were soon revealed to be attempts to influence or control my decisions. I cried, prayed, called my boyfriend and family for support but the only support I could get was that from a sweet little nun at the hospital. She was also a nurse who took care of me. Her name was Sue and I can still recall the sweet calmness of her voice. She told me that man will disappoint you but our Heavenly Father never would. She prayed with me, in spite of the fact that I was a murderer in God's eyes, my eyes and those of my family. Sue just loved me and talked to me about the rape, my virginity and choices I had made. She told me that my virginity was stolen from me and that my choice to open the apartment door was not an act of my giving it away. That statement changed everything for me. My thinking changed.

The brain surgery was completed. My face, eyes and nose were severely swollen and black from bruising but the pressure in my head seemed to be lessened. I still had no vision but decisions were made, it was over and I had a peace in my heart that I had been forgiven. Forgiven by God yes, but it took me many years to forgive myself and come to accept the decisions that I made.

Two weeks later, I returned to my apartment with some vision. The doctors said that as the swelling subsides, more vision should be restored. I was excited and ready to make some serious changes in my life. Guess who showed back up. My fiancé. Yeah, the one that packed up and skipped out. Now that I wasn't sick anymore, or pregnant I might add, he loved me again. *Get out!* I genuinely loved him so it took me two more years to totally unload him from my life but I never had any sexual activity with him again.

My family was quick to spread gossip. To them, my being a "whore" was validated by these events and choices; as well as in the minds of their circles of influence. I was a good girl… I didn't drink alcohol, didn't smoke, didn't do drugs, wasn't sexually promiscuous, was going to college for my second degree, genuinely loved God and was involved with my church. It didn't matter to them. I was the one who shamed their family and the family dynamic was set. The family wasn't ready for what was getting ready to come to light but it was coming.

CHAPTER 14

Within a month, my mother was diagnosed with a rare type of breast cancer and being carted all over the US for treatments that weren't working. She was given three months to live but continued to fight for her life for nearly three years.

We all took turns helping her and spending time with her. I continued finishing my Bachelor's degree but kept close tabs on Mom, every day. One day she would be on her deathbed and the next, she'd be up doing her taxes. She was such a fighter and wanted to live. She continued to be detached and cold to me emotionally, making sure that when I was in the house, everyone guarded their purses. I wanted nothing more than to make amends and have some sort of relationship with her, before her passing, but she was a hard nut to crack. On one hand, she was generous, caring, compassionate and loving with others but not the same with me. I spent untold amounts of time trying to get to sleep at night and having my mind race though ideas, as to what I did to make her dislike me so. I genuinely couldn't come up with much of anything.

Certain visits were difficult when she'd get on the topic of how she got cancer. She really felt that I was the reason for her getting sick. I came along so late in life that they felt pressured to create a better life for me so they got themselves in financial deep water with the nursing homes and therefore had to make it work. This I understood, but when she said that if I had only shut my mouth and went along with everything, she wouldn't have been so stressed and gotten cancer. So, in her mind, I gave her cancer and she would really take it out on me, during some visits. So much so, that some visits were cut really short. I knew better than this *but* I loved my mother dearly. Could I have been responsible for her dying now? After all my love does kill!

Two months before her passing, my mother was having a good day and getting around quite well. She asked me, "If you could do anything with me before I die, what would it be?" My answer was to go to the park and feed the ducks together. So, she dragged herself up, covered up her nightgown with her full length mink coat and slowly made her way to the car. We drove three blocks to the park and spent twenty minutes feeding the ducks together, holding hands, smiling at one another and peacefully being a Mommy and her little girl. I felt so much joy and she seemed to also. She pointed out a monarch butterfly and we both smiled. She told me to always watch for butterflies because it would be her; coming by to say hi and let me know that I'm not alone. I waited twenty-one years for this interaction, twenty-one years. Thank you, God, for this twenty minute gift. We returned home, were greeted by my father who quickly helped my mother back into bed. He told me, with a tear in his eye, that he had never seen her look so happy and peaceful. He asked me what happened. I told him and he said, "That's it?"

That's it, Dad... my Mother was my Mama!

Two weeks before my mother died, she began to seek quiet, private conversations with me. Desperate for more mother / daughter time, I agreed. I took off of work and school and just stayed with her. She had changed, was different, resolved to her fate, wanting resolution! She liked her hands and legs massaged and then she wanted her nails painted a pale pink color. I did as she asked and each day I began to change the color on her nails. At one point she was unable to move her arms, because of so much fluid buildup, so I saw the chance to be in control. I took out my *jezebel* red and went to town. As I finished, she opened her eyes and just started to roar in laughter. She loved it and we both laughed for what seemed like an eternity. It was fun laughing with my mama.

The next day, she began to talk about her life before I was born. She told me that she and Daddy were trying to adopt a set of twins, which had red hair. They were a little older but that's what she wanted because she didn't want to deal with an infant, was too old to have children and having a baby at her "old age" was asking for trouble. People in their forties gave birth to babies with severe defects of some sort and she couldn't have that. She was told that she was in menopause, so she was shocked to find that she was pregnant with me. She began to cry, telling me that she was so scared of what people would think and how our family would be treated if the baby was retarded or disabled. She said she hadn't been thinking clearly but knew that she didn't want to carry a child. What she told me next shocked me beyond belief. She began to sob and through her tears, she asked me to forgive her. I asked, "What for?"

She replied, "Because I tried to get rid of you myself."

I was confused. What do you mean you tried to, "get rid me?" She refused to give me details but talked about my aunt who worked at a state hospital and how she had access to things that would terminate a pregnancy. She sobbed and I cried with her; partially because she was so upset and partially because I was in shock over what I was hearing.

She kept repeating, "It didn't work, it didn't work." She said that once she realized it hadn't worked, she tried to get her sister to help her try again, but her sister refused. She said that she hated her sister because she wouldn't help her again and this became the reason for their lifetime rift. I always wondered why there were such bad feelings between the two, but how could anyone ever guess something like this?

Once she was resolved to the fact that she would be having a baby, they cancelled the adoption of the twins and she began to prepare for an infant, me. She told me that she did try to love me during her pregnancy and that she grew to love me after I was born. She said that it was difficult because she was so old and set in her ways, and that pregnancy and infancy changed her life more than she was prepared for. She also shared that my siblings loved me, however, there was a strong sense of jealousy towards me, because my parents were able to give me more financially than they could provide when my brother and sister were children. They were no longer the center of attention and my arrival changed their lives more than they were prepared for to.

She said I was her miracle baby. I remember growing up hearing that, but never knew what that meant. Now, I understand, it was a miracle that I survived the termination attempt.

I asked her who knew about what she tried to do and she said nobody; "Not even your father, just your aunt." She told me that she gave up her figure for me, her freedom because she had to go to work in the nursing homes for added income and now her life, because the stress of having me has given her cancer. She went on and on, asking for forgiveness for all of the things that she did, didn't do and should have done. She apologized for not protecting me, for allowing others to hurt me, for not being affectionate and being unkind at times. Explaining that my brother had been horrifically sexually abused by a grandfather, when he was a small boy, and so was my sister, she revealed. More family secrets revealed. She felt that by holding my brother accountable would further damage him. (I kept thinking if she wondered about the damage I endured) We talked about the fact that if she would have held him accountable, others may not have been harmed. The cycle was allowed to continue, but it was stopping with me! I wanted to dedicate my life to helping others, not hurting them and when I shared that, she began to cry. Tears from both of us flooded the room for the next week or so. We talked about everything and my childhood became crystal clear; aspects clicking into place like dominos falling in line. Things that I couldn't piece together for anything, suddenly slipped into place.

Thank you, Mama for loving me, for the affection you showed during those short two weeks and the acceptance you gave me, in forgiving me for my mistakes. The last two weeks of your life were filled with all of the things I longed for my whole life!

As I was rubbing her legs, they began to turn blue. She was passing but I didn't want her to go. Don't leave me, Mama. I just got you, I thought! But I leaned down and whispered in her ear, "It's okay, Mama, I'll be okay. I'm safe. It's okay to go. Jesus awaits you." She opened up her eyes, scanned the room filled with loved ones and settled back to my eyes, smiled, and through her cancer-ridden lips, she said that she loved me as she took her last breath.

Once again, my heart was broken. The mother I had always longed for, I had gotten; only to lose her! The pain in my chest was more than I could bear! I ran out of the house and began to run! I ran for hours, sobbing aloud with no destination, just running! How much can someone endure and still maintain sanity, let alone still love God? All questions I asked through my tears. I ran until I couldn't walk any further. I found myself in the middle of a cornfield, unsure of my location which made me angry. I began to wildly swing my arms and legs in a fit of rage and that day, I took twenty one years of pain, anger and revenge out on a crop of corn. I think it was my brother-in-law who found me that day, lovingly comforted me and took me home. He was always kind to me, reasonable, encouraging and I looked up to him as my "big brother".

The day after her passing, I went to the funeral home and talked to the director. I explained what I wanted to do. He had a shocked look on his face and quickly called my father and siblings. My siblings were adamant that I have no chance to do what I am wanting but my father said yes. He thought it was morbid but agreed if that was something I wanted to do. It was okay with him, so I did. The last gift I could ever give my mother was to do her nails for her. So I cleaned off the bright red, all the while talking to her and painted them with her favorite pale pink polish. I thought heaven might appreciate the pink better than the jezebel red Mom; hope you approve.

We buried her the very next day in a beautiful light pink dress and although I was wrought with grief, I felt this unstated, strange sense of relief. The daily conflicts and games I'd known most of my life, were over. No more guilt trips, head-games, manipulation for control, and constant seeking for her approval. Something I could have never put into words then, because the words alone would have produced exorbitant amounts of guilt, guilt that I wasn't willing to make my own and guilt I never have taken on.

That day I made a decision to build my own motherhood on what my mother taught me *not* to do during the first twenty one years of my life, and what to do from the last two weeks of her life; especially the twenty minutes in the park.

Nearly thirty years later… Mama, I can still feel your hand in mine as we stroll along feeding the ducks. I can feel your fingertip wipe my tears as I type these words and I can see the tenderness in your eyes as you forgive and seek forgiveness. I love you, Mama and pray that your walks with Jesus, on streets of gold, are as joyous as our walk in the park.

Mother was gone. Father remained but in a state of shock, disbelief and complete grief; we all were! The strong woman, who seemed to never quit or give up, had. Her body had quit, given up! The rest of us had to pick up and somehow go on; forging a new reality for our futures.

Dad drew strength from the hospice worker who always seemed to be there for him. She was a tiny petite woman with a kind smile, gentle touch and warm hug. Her words comforted and her never-ending presence began to grow on us all. I returned to college classes, finishing up my final requirements for my second degree, my siblings returned to work and their families and my father struggled through each day, as if it needed to be the last day of his life. He continued to take solace in the hospice worker and a friendship quickly grew. I was glad that he found someone that he could totally open up and talk to, giving him a reason to hang on! That dear friendship remained intact for the next twenty plus years; until dementia demanded she be put in a home, close to her family but far from my father.

Over forty years with the same woman, a strong, intelligent, hard-working, domineering woman; that none other could ever compare to. How does one survive such a loss? One breath at a time.

CHAPTER 15

My father was struggling so much, that I offered to move in with him for a short period of time. I only had a short time left of college and wanted to get closer to him. In a blink of an eye, I was back under the same roof as the man who beat me to a pulp many years before. He was a different man now; he had been beaten now and now was the time for me to walk the talk of compassion, forgiveness and love, so I did. We cried together, held hands, hugged and kept each other company, during the dark evenings and early mornings.

One morning my father asked if I wanted to go to Dunkin Donuts, for coffee and a donut. I remember him taking me there when I was a little girl. I'd eat so many Boston cream-filled donuts and spin around on the stool so fast that he'd have to pull the car over on the way home, so I could throw up over and over. Maybe that's why we stopped going there. I agreed to join him and as we were sitting at a table, he began to open up and share some things. He asked me why I was so angry with him. Angry at him? Wow, I was confused. I'd grown up seeing him with this underlying rage, which could present itself at any given time. When I shared with him this thought and my experience, he began to tell me that he hated my brother. I had no idea he felt that way but he continued to explain. He said that my brother put he, and my mother through hell, before I ever came along. Dad talked about the time my brother set the neighbor's crop on fire. Dad was trying to put it out and in turn, his hairline was singed-off and never re-grew. Many examples were given, of how my brother stressed my parents and got my father into conflicts with neighbors. As he proceeded, the rage began to surface in his voice and on his face. He called him the "rottenest little sucker that ever lived." He said he grew to hate him and could never shake the hatred; even after forty years. I saw this in his adult interactions with my brother too, but always thought it was his anger towards me coming out towards others – which always rendered a bit of guilt, in that, my crap was being cast upon others. More family secrets revealed. He shared that he felt that my siblings were unkind, judgmental and critical of me, because they were jealous of me. An idea that I must admit I struggle with to this day. What about me is worthy of anyone's jealousy? Things I never knew were being shared. Another parent, another private conversation, open hearts, open minds; life-changing. My father continued, by asking me again why I was so angry with him. I felt safe enough to share my feelings and the effects of my childhood. I kept certain information vague about my brother and grandfather (not knowing what he was aware of, but assuming he knew as my mother did) but shared the effects it all had on my life. We talked about the night of the beating, my mother's role and how all of this could have been avoided from the start of my life. I chose not to share what my mother told me about, because her death was too fresh and in no way did I want him to perceive me as talking badly about her. My father began to cry and right there in the middle of Dunkin Donuts, he got on his knees, took me by the hands and began to ask for my forgiveness. Through an endless stream of vocal tears, he laid his head in my lap and begged for forgiveness. I stroked his hair and through tears of my own, I told him that I had already forgiven him many years ago. This seemed to make him cry harder and when I said that it was time he forgave my brother and himself, he began to sob. We both stayed in that position, crying aloud for quite some time, in the presence of others and the healing began. It was over! A new relationship was being forged; a new beginning.

CHAPTER 16

During the next four months, many things happened to solidify my new relationship with my father, but other things occurred that further divided me from my siblings. Untruths were gossiped about me, to their friends and those in our community. They would hold family get-togethers in which I wasn't invited, accused me of partaking in alcohol and illegal substances, sexual promiscuity and even go as far as sharing these untruths with their young children / teenagers, so as to influence them to distance themselves from me. I adored my nieces and nephews and still do. My father would stand up to them, on my behalf, and they would then call me and invite me last minute with some half-cocked tone of voice. I would stand up for myself and attend, only to be shunned, whispered about, laughed and my sister always made it a point to remind everyone that I had arrived, so everyone watch your pocketbooks. *Wow, my sister had become my mother, or had she been like this all along and I just didn't notice?* I was a twenty one year old girl that had just lost her mother. I know she was their mother too but all of this behavior was not justified by their grief. When I tried to lovingly talk about it with them, they would laugh at me, mock me and make fun to the point that I would begin to stutter and stammer. This made me angry and frustrated so I stopped the attempts. The gossip and defamation of my character continued. Nothing was going to change; that was clear. The buffer and glue that held our family together had died. Dad's attempts to stand up for me were for naught, because my siblings just became more covert in their behavior and learned not to say anything about me to Dad.

I finished my college requirements and graduated with my second degree. My father was so proud that I was the first family member, in the history of our family, to ever go to a four year college, let alone graduate in five years with two degrees that normally take six to complete. He sweetly offered to throw me a graduation party and I was so honored at his offer, that although I didn't know who to invite, I agreed. We invited neighbors, friends of my parents, some of my college friends, professors that I had grown close to and of course my siblings. I wanted everyone to enjoy this time of fellowship so the party was set.

The party began and the turnout was better than I expected. With thirty to thirty five present, catered food and a beautiful atmosphere; everyone seemed to be enjoying one another and having fun. While my dad and I were in the kitchen talking to the staff, some of our guests came in to wish me well but stated that they had to be leaving. I was confused. The party had just started fifteen minutes ago and you're already leaving. When I asked why, I was told by all three couples that they were hearing things that were disturbing. My dad inquired and they proceeded to reluctantly open up and share that my siblings and their spouses were sitting in the large room, talking loudly and making unloving remarks about me. In fact, making fun of the fact that it took me five years to get a four year degree and my degree was in drinking alcohol, sleeping around and prostitution. They reported that they were laughing out loud and saying much more, that everyone in the room could clearly hear. My head dropped and I wanted to hide. I felt a surge of anger and I lifted my head and apologized to my guests for my sibling's childish behavior and asked them to please stay. They all agreed that they couldn't stand the thought of staying but that they loved me and gave me good wishes. Because these were friends of my fathers and longtime neighbors of my parents, I trusted the credibility of what they were saying. As my guests left, I looked at my father, with eyes that I am sure spoke volumes. "How do I handle this one, Pop?" I said.

"This is how I'm treated all of the time; they just don't let you see it anymore." The rage hit his face and my father exited the room, with me in hand, confronted my siblings and their spouses and demand that they leave the event. They acted surprised, offended and self-righteous, but what was new. I still, to this day, am unaware as to whether or not my sister's husband was part of that ordeal or if he just allowed it to continue. He had always treated me with love, respect and kindness and many years later I was told by a credible source that his kindness made my sister angry and uneasy. I have always loved him like a brother and always appreciated his encouragement, love and support. Regardless, I can only imagine what he's had to put up with all of these years.

The turmoil with my siblings came to an all time high and I couldn't take it much longer. I would go to grocery stores and check out through a line where the cashier was a friend of my sisters. As I passed through the line, I would hear the cashier call me a "whore". This wasn't going to get better, it's only going to get worse. Are they trying to make me crazy? Take my life? Run away again? Leave town? What was their agenda? Did they want me out of Dad's life? Were they jealous? I couldn't figure it out, just as I couldn't figure out why my mother was indifferent and unloving to me as a child. Maybe this wasn't really about me or something I had done at all. Maybe it was all about them! My sister had started to treat me as the mother of my childhood and my brother was either indifferent or abusive; as she was. Regardless, I wasn't going to spend the next twenty one years of my life trying to get their acceptance, approval, love and affection. I was done! I deserved better and I was going to get it!

CHAPTER 17

When I got an offer from my old fiancé to move out to the East Coast with him, I made my boundaries very clear to him, but jumped at the chance. I went for a visit, applied for graduate school while I was there, and was immediately accepted. Wheels were in motion. I returned to Illinois, sold nearly everything I had accumulated, bought a truck and packed only those things that were highly important to me. If I could have packed my father, I would have. There was no way he would ever leave but I knew I couldn't stay. My siblings were vicious and it wasn't fair to have my father put in the middle, so I had to go. My heart was exhilarated in one sense but on another plane, my heart was breaking. I had just found and then lost my mother, established a new relationship with my father and now leaving that too, but it was clear that my siblings would make my life hell if I stayed. Fight or flight... I fought and it got me nowhere so now it was time to leave.

Driving to the outside city limits, my father drove close to my bumper; seeing me off. I pulled the truck over at the city limits sign and we both got out. We tightly embraced, I took his face in my hands and I said, "I love you so much Daddy but I just can't stay, it's not you."

He said, "I know, honey but I don't know what to do to change your brother and sister." I understood that his hands were tied and he understood that I didn't want this to make his life more difficult. My going was best for us both. We both tearfully held each other and I told him that I would come back to visit and I welcomed him to come visit me, but I will never return for longer than forty eight hours. We both wept, as we were illegally parked, but there was a peaceful understanding that was established that day. I can still feel the pain in my chest, as I drove away and onto my new life.

I arrived in Virginia, moved into my ex-fiance's apartment and started graduate school. Within five weeks, I had acquired a full-time job in my field of study, continued with full-time graduate courses and moved into my own apartment. Within one year, I had moved up in the company, gotten a 4.0 grade point average and created a life filled with friends, laughter, financial independence and travel.

I started returning home to Chicago-land, for a weekend here and there, to visit Dad. The second my sister heard I was in town, she would make her presence known. She tried to be friendly and welcoming which would temporarily suck me in, until her claws would emerge. I was right. Within forty eight hours, conflict would begin and I left town. I didn't want anything to do with it and although I was worth standing up for, she wasn't worth fighting with. Funny but when someone comes to your door every Friday night at six p.m. and the second you open the door they punch you in the kisser, eventually you stop opening the door or start punching them before they land one on you. Or you just find yourself not home at 6 p. m. Either way, I was not giving her viciousness any legs to stand on.

Two years passed, years filled with great travel, amazing income, perfect grades and a new life. My sister and her husband wanted to come see me. This was intriguing to me because they were putting forth effort, their dime and their time. Surely by now they would see that I am someone worthy of getting to know, lovable, loving and worthy of their acceptance; so they came. I put them up in my guest bedroom, fully stocked with antiques I had acquired and my home was beautiful, warm and welcoming. Working full time has many benefits and I was a smart girl in finding deals and restoring old pieces, so my home was quite nice and I had even acquired a newer vehicle. I decided I would take time off of work and it was a visit that arrived between semesters so it was perfectly timed.

CHAPTER 18

After several days, of what I thought was a nice visit, filled with many complimentary comments on my home, wardrobe and vehicle, my sister and her husband left. I went back to my life as usual; busy beyond belief as the new semester was about to begin and I was going to be taking twenty one hours of graduate hours plus working full time. I did it and with good grades.

Within a few weeks of my sisters' return, I started hearing things from back home. Friends from high school would call me and say that they heard. You heard *what?* Oh my Lord, the gossip and defamation continues. I was beyond livid and it was a fight worth fighting, so I packed a bag, used my paid vacation, rescheduled exams and drove twelve hours non-stop to return home. Within seconds of my arrival, I sat down with my father, who was acting quite strange and distant towards me. When I finally got it out of him what was bothering him, he informed me that my brother had told him that he heard I was prostituting and selling drugs to live. I couldn't believe what I was hearing!

I became outraged and demanded that we call a family meeting immediately. I reassured my father that this was a complete and utter lie and he knew I was speaking the truth, so he got on the phone and the meeting was set.

When my brother and sister arrived, they had a troubled look on their face. What was going on, I'm sure they wondered, as my father told them nothing in advance. They didn't even know that I was in town, so they were quite surprised. My sister said, "Dad what's wrong; what's happened?" Dad didn't reply but as I walked into the room, both my sister and brothers faces dropped and my brother quickly acquired a sheepish grin. These are people in their mid forties behaving like this. I sat down and Dad took charge. He asked my brother to repeat what he had told him earlier that week.

My brother admitted saying this to my father but quickly followed with, "But your sister returned home from visiting you and told me that."

I spoke up and asked if he believed such a thing?

He said, "Why would I ever doubt what she was saying?" (a grin on his face). I turned, faced my sister and just looked at her.

She quickly said, "You're living better than me and I'm almost twenty years older than you." There it was, wow! She said she couldn't figure out how I could do it and still have time / money to afford quick trips back to see Dad so often. My brother blamed my sister and she was trying to cover her backside; to no end. I wasn't having it. They were both trying to cut me down, in hopes of elevating themselves and I just wasn't having it! I remember thinking that if I didn't stand up now, I would never take a stand for anything. I spoke to them in a way that would shame anyone who was spreading malicious gossip; let alone about their own sister… and without one stitch of truth to this tapestry of lies. My parents were right and that was clear. They were jealous. Of what I was still unsure of but what I did know, they would stop at nothing to undermine my character, my relationship with my father and my reputation. I informed them that they would have to answer to God for this but that I will never forget the evil they have spoken and spread. I assured them that I have never done drugs, do not drink alcohol, am not sexually active, do not exploit myself or others, do not make money via any illegal means and would never invite either of them as guests into my home again.

It's now over twenty five years later and I never have to date. I do believe things can change and with God all things are possible *(Matthew 19:26)*. However, my home is my safe haven and I never invite the devil into my home *(1 Peter 5:8 – "Be of sober spirit, be on the alert. Your adversary, the devil, prowls around like a roaring lion, seeking someone to devour." – NASB)*. Being the keeper of brick walls is not what we are called to do, but being the gate-keeper of a chain-link fence, where others can be touched, conversed with and invited in, is a healthy thing! Be careful who you allow in and open the gate for; there are many wolves in sheep's clothing, talking a good talk but don't walk the talk.

Over the years, attempts have been made on my behalf, to no avail. The jealousy remains on their part even though they are well into their late sixties and they continue to live in denial of their own survived childhood abuse. My attempts halted, when my children were little and venomous attempts were made to undermine my relationship with them.

To this day, an apology has never come from my siblings. Not for the inappropriate touch, not for the false accusations, not for the defamation of my character, not for the humiliation, not for the unkind manner in which I was treated; not for anything. Sad part is, I choose to still love them and pray for them daily and that alone releases me from the bondage of anger and resentment, that I once walked in. A simple apology would have made all of the difference in the world, by I forgave them long ago. *"Forgiveness is the fragrance that the violet sheds on the heel that has crushed it." – Mark Twain.*

Anger, resentment and family secrets are the toxins that feed on what could be, eat away what should be and sever the strings that bind. Open honesty, taking ownership and forgiveness are the tools the physician uses to heal the hearts involved. The patients have to be willing to be healed and allow themselves the gift of vulnerability and honest self-evaluation. Without this; one doesn't get better, they get bitter!

Patterns we learn and live have astronomical rippling effects. It's time for a thought revolution. A revival of our mind!

A woman now, I stood on my own, confronted the demons of my past and feeling confident to protect me and mine, I returned to graduate school and work. My life anew begins.

PART 3

The New Walk

CHAPTER 19

A new life has truly begun. I am walking with a spring in my step by this point. I felt like a woman now for the first time. So much had happened in such a short amount of time. For the next two years, there were no interruptions to my education or stability, although I had re-growths of the brain tumor. As long as I kept my stress down and continued medication; all was well.

After nearly two years, I received an evaluation from my doctor that disturbed me. I was told that my cycle irregularity was due to severe scar tissue; more than likely from the rape and medical abortion. The likelihood of ever having children was next to nothing. Although I didn't see myself as having children or even wanting children in the near future, it disturbed me. Once again, my past was haunting my present and future. Hearing this felt as if my choice to ever have children was being taken from me. I found it ironic that the act of utilizing my "choice" was leaving me with no choices. After reasoning out my thoughts and feelings with counselors, pastors, friends and much prayer, I decided to look into fertility options. After all, I was emotionally stable, financially stable, educated and had the insurance and funds to put forth. The process began.

I spent the next eighteen months alternating between graduate classes, traveling the world with my job, researching, interviewing doctors and packing away money. I bought a condo, refurbished it and began buying baby items. I believed the process would begin and end successfully so why not prepare wisely. Finally decisions were made, the doctor, the type of process, the donor and the date!

Month after month, my cycle would start! No success! My belief stayed intact but I was regularly reminded that my chances are next to nil. <u>I'm not listening</u>! Again and again, my cycle starts! The emotional rollercoaster that accompanied this process was profound. Funds were running out, options were dwindling, I was becoming emotionally raw! I went in for my last procedure, and said thank you to the staff, because I just *knew* this was going to be the one that took! For days I waited with bated breath. I was *so* excited I had trouble sleeping, eating and focusing on even the slightest thing. Omigosh, here it is, the buildup was great. I thought, tomorrow morning I take the in home pregnancy test! I am *so* excited! In the middle of the night I awoke from cramps, got up to use the toilet and my cycle started! There were small amounts but that made it clear to me. I began to cry. Totally disappointed, deflated and distraught, because there wasn't any money left and I was exhausted. It was over; I was done! The next morning I called the doctor and informed them. They were disappointed for me, but that's life, as the girl on the other end reminded me. Argh!

Two days later, I noticed that my cycle had ended, which was strange. Usually Rosie and her god-blasted sisters overstayed their welcome, but this month was different. It's probably just the break God knew I needed and I just laughed. A week later, I went to the doctor for my case-closing appointment. The doctor walked into the room and sat down. We began to talk and he stopped me in mid-sentence. He said, "You have a glow about yourself."

I laughed and said, "Yeah, that's from throwing up all night from a plate of bad Chinese food."

He said he'd be right back and returned with a nurse. I gave a urine sample and they quickly disappeared. A few moments later, the doctor and his whole office of staff came into the room. I was confused but sat quietly. The doctor said, "Mitsey, you're going to be a mama!"

Shocked, I said, "What?"

He repeated it and everyone began to cheer. I couldn't believe it, but my cycle. He quickly told me that it was common for there to be spotting and cramping upon implantation. So I asked, "Does that mean that when I was awakened with cramping and bloodspots, the baby was implanting itself into the lining of my uterus? Is that what I'm hearing you say?"

He said, "Yes," and joy flooded my soul and my tears flooded the floor! Everyone was crying with me. The likelihood of that little one finding its way to the tiny place that was not damaged by scar tissue, was a miracle. This baby was *my* miracle baby but I wanted this so very badly! I still had a home pregnancy test in my purse and asked if I could dip it and keep it for memories. That was the most beautiful day of my life! Morning sickness was gone in no time, I ate healthily, only drank water, craved shaved ice, got plenty of rest and sang songs to this miracle growing within. Within a month, it hit me!

I had to tell my family. I hadn't even discussed any of this with my father! Oh my. How is it that this hadn't even crossed my mind throughout this whole process? This would be perceived as my playing God and wouldn't go over well at *all*! Panic set in and within seconds I reverted to a little girl again, worrying about losing approval, acceptance, affection, love and falling from grace. How would I approach this? How can I tell him and maintain the pride he had in me, the love he had for me and the stamp of approval he had given me? I had the solution. I was going to lie! That's what I did. I told my father that I fell in love and got swept away, etc. Although he wasn't happy at all and I'm sure his pride was hurt, he seemed to act sympathetically. Whew, okay that was over but wait, I had reacted to emotions of panic and handled it from that place of a little girl. I didn't think it through. Now what do I do? So I sat on it. Quickly the news spread to my siblings, who reveled in the new gossip. I let it sit but eventually would have to do something. What a mess I've started now. Knee jerk reactions to old messages!

CHAPTER 20

Within two days, I was informed that there was another growth on my brain and my new doctor told me that this tumor was different and was more than likely malignant! Oh dear God, please don't allow this to happen again. I panicked and spent the next couple of days on my knees. You know the routine, pregnant plus tumor, termination. *No*, it wasn't going to happen again! God could take us both home, before I would be faced to make a decision like that again.

I scheduled appointments with specialists and met with the dean of the college at my graduate school. I was in the home stretch but they needed to know what I was facing. I was wrought with emotion; partially due to raging hormones I'm sure, but nevertheless, I was a mess.

After two agonizing weeks and several specialists, good news came. It was not malignant but the same type of tumor that I had dealt with for years. What relief. I felt at least this was familiar. Wait, panic struck again because it still meant making a decision to terminate and I tearfully refused! Flat out refused! The doctor calmed me down and informed me that a new medication had been released that helps to control the hormones that were overproducing and cause the tumors and in turn should help to shrink it! I cried for joy and agreed to do anything they told me to do! I went on a strict regimen of meds and diet and things began to improve. Back on track and healthy baby still in tow!

I had started dating someone new that was vying for my attention to the fullest. He seemed to be a nice guy and came from what appeared to be a nice family. He pursued me even though I fully informed him of the choices I'd made and the circumstances I had created, along with the health challenges I'd had. He was thrilled at the idea and it seemed to endear him to me even more. This was not the effect I was going for. I thought for sure that my being with child, by choice, and also sick, would send him running for the hills, but it didn't. He said he couldn't have children, was found sterile and the idea thrilled him. The harder I tried to push him away, the more he pursued. Flowers, cards, notes on my car window, spontaneous lunch deliveries at work; today they would call it stalking but I saw it as determined infatuation. Over time he wore me down, won me over and we were engaged six months later. He fully respected my boundaries, treated me like a queen and never pushed for more. He attended church with me, liked my friends and they liked him. His family loved me, accepted me and appeared to be thrilled. I didn't see any red flags, or maybe I chose not to see any.

Our relationship grew closer and so did that with his family. We celebrated our first Christmas together and they treated me as if I was already their daughter. I was stunned by their generosity, kindness and welcoming spirits. They were aware of everything and openly accepted the whole idea. They were already planning baby showers along with wedding events. Dress shopping, along with nursery shopping; what a strange turn of events but one that was joyfully welcomed. His mother soon became a mother figure to me. We grew so incredibly close and she began to share things in a casual way, that weren't picked up by me for what they really were… warnings! I was so caught up in everything happening that I genuinely didn't see what she was attempting to do. I see now that in her being straightforward would have felt like a betrayal to her son but it sure could have saved a great deal of heartache if she had. Nevertheless, planning continued, dresses purchased, nursery painted and engagement party held. Due date fast approaching and I was having a baby boy! A *boy?* What did the doctor mean when he said that he had been wrong? Hurry, repaint the nursery! Off to the mall to exchange colors… *of everything*!

CHAPTER 21

Clean up on aisle 10! You've got to be kidding. The mall was packed with people, everyone is looking at me and began to clap. I started laughing and clapping while looking at the lady standing next to me. Nobody bought it, so I just began making comments that sparked laughter in others. "Yes, I make a splash wherever I go"... and so forth. What a rush... *what a mess*! I calmly exited the mall, being ever so clever; using my bags to cover the fact that I looked like I'd just peed myself.

Stopping home to pick up my hospital bag, take a shower, do my hair and makeup; yes, judge me if you want but I wanted to start this process looking and feeling pretty. Phone calls made, people panicking to reach me and yet I felt the strangest sense of peace and joy that I've even felt. My future mother-in-law drove me to the hospital and my fiancé "John" met us there, carrying a beautiful bouquet of flowers and a huge gift bag from Macy's. Yeah, that's right; he was playing it smart. It was amazing to think about. Here I am going into labor with essentially another man's baby; even though the donor would never have known but this man and his family were just as excited, as if this child was his. It was very reassuring of the affection I felt and the acceptance I needed. The flowers were arranged and the elegant flowing white lace gown set, from Macy's, adorned my huge belly. By goodness, I looked and felt beautiful. I was SO excited to meet this little man and already had a litany of names listed for my choosing. What name would I settle on? What name would he look like? Little did I realize that over thirty-six hours of labor would leave me looking like I'd been through WW3. My hair was screwed up, raccoon eyes adorned my face, a gown that was no longer white, flower vase knocked off of the nightstand, a broken collar bone, stitches in places that I didn't even know I owned and a beautiful 7 pound 8 ounce baby boy. I was overjoyed, as my fiancé cut the cord and laid my precious little man on my chest. Tears of joy flooded my eyes as I prayed over him; thanking God for my miracle baby. He was healthy, strong and perfect! I was put on high doses of Demerol due to some complications, which turned out to be another blessing. When my son was born, my body shed all of the scar tissue, during the birthing process. The doctors were in awe and I was overwhelmed with emotion and pain. It was almost as if my baby son had healed the past. So incredibly strange but everything felt new, fresh and restored.

The next day, I was holding my new son and talking with him; yes he was speaking. His eyes spoke volumes, full of life and love. I asked him to pick his name, so as I went down the list and I watched for his head to move, facial expressions or any sign of emotion. I saw something with every single name I mentioned all five! So I gave him *all* five of the names! His first name and the rest would be initials, as his middle name. I've always blamed that one on the Demerol, what's a girl to do! No, I did not give him my fiancé's last name or put him on the birth certificate, which proved to be the best decision possible, in the long run. His family wasn't happy about that, but we weren't even married yet. I saw this decision as responsible and level-headed. My son, "Jonathan" was accepted as one of their own and the days to follow were filled with love, joy, happiness, tenderness, tears and out-of-state unexpected company.

Yes, my father and sister showed up. As soon as I saw them I was happy, until the guilt of my lie came into focus. My fiancé knew of my error but his family did not. No, we never told them but each time my father held "Jonathan", I felt overwrought with guilt. I *had* to make this right and couldn't stand it much longer. I wanted to live in truth; not the dysfunction of lies and secrecy, so I decided to allow myself to be vulnerable and asked to speak to my father alone. My sister put out some lip but Dad agreed. Holding my son, I proceeded to tell my father that I had made a mistake; a mistake that I made, directly out of knee jerk reactions to fear. He lovingly listened and said that I could tell him anything. I thought, I know I can tell you anything Daddy but what price will I end up paying and how will this innocent child pay? I continued to tell him that I am deeply concerned to reveal the truth because I don't want him to lose pride in me, stop loving my son or judge my choices. My sister walked in the room and he pressed me, so I told him. Immediately, my sister smiled and started in… my father didn't stop her but had this look of complete disappointment on his face, as he lowered his head. My heart was aching. He said, "You played God and took life into your own hands, again. Why couldn't you wait until you were married? Why did you conceive a baby in a lab versus love?"

I stopped him immediately and said, "Yes, I spent my last bit of savings to do it and yes, I took steps that are against what you believe in but let's get one thing straight! I did this out of nothing *but* love and will not allow you or anyone else to make this process dirty or sterile of emotion. I have more love for this little man than I've ever felt for anyone!" I apologized for my lie but I refused to apologize for my timing and technique chosen. I wanted to smack the smug look off of my sister's face and beg my father for forgiveness… should I have just let them continue to think that I just got knocked up? Why is it that they could forgive that idea faster than an adult woman, making an adult decision, to plan for parenthood and seek techniques that would allow that to happen. Why would a one night stand be an act that wouldn't affect his pride but this did? How ridiculous and I was angry at myself for ever falling prey to the fear of my childhood, breaching my integrity with dishonesty…never again. From that point forward, I would be straightforwardly honest; regardless of the cost. If I'm not right with myself and right with God, then at the end of the day, things just aren't right and nothing goes right!

My father and my sister left for Illinois. I was joyful, sad, peaceful, angry and now that everyone had gone back to their daily lives, I was learning how to be a mother, meeting daily needs on every level. I loved being a mommy and I was good at it. Amazing love was exchanged between the two of us. Time passed, "Jonathan" grew like crazy and yet, there was no news or contact from home. Things weren't the same with my father and 22+ years later; still aren't.

CHAPTER 22

Our wedding took place six months after "Jonathan" was born. My father said that he wouldn't give me away, unless we held it in my home town and my sister was my matron-of-honor. By this time, I was so anxious to have things restored with my father that I agreed to his demands, so off to Chicago we went.

Two nights before the wedding, my fiancé and I were to meet with the pastor and have some pre-marital counseling. We agreed to meet at the church at 6:00 p.m. but my fiancé never showed. Where was he? What was he doing? I was vacillating between worry, anger, sadness, embarrassment and panic. Had he changed his mind? What was going on? After not hearing from him or his family all night, I was resolved with the idea of not getting married to this man. How dare he not show, contact me or have his family contact me. This was the first red flag! My sister arrived to my dad's house in the morning, with news. How did she get news or even know this was happening. She proceeds to tell me that her teenage children took him out the night before and they were bar-hopping. What? I didn't believe a word of this because I had never seen him take alcohol and the only time I ever saw him in a bar was one night when we wanted to play pool, while dating. Could this be my sister's doing! I didn't trust her for anything and why would her children have any interest in taking him out. I was off the charts angry but I respectfully listened. She went on to tell me how they reported back to her that he was doing other types of drugs too, which is when I demanded she stop. She will stop at nothing to cause me pain, grief, unhappiness, to look badly in Dad's eyes and be the brunt of my defaming gossip. Within minutes, my fiancé arrived and was panic-stricken. He took me by the shoulders and began to cry. He showed such incredible remorse, as he explained that my sister's kids took him out the afternoon before and wanted to celebrate with a little afternoon bachelor party. They went to a bar and they started buying shots. He said he told them that he could only have one or two since he was meeting me at the church later that day and didn't want to have alcohol on his breath. He expressed feeling pressure to accept their hospitality but one thing led to another and they were at another bar. The alcohol took over his judgment and he lost track of time. He denied doing any other drugs and said that he woke up in his hotel room this morning sick, and panicked when he realized he had missed our appointment with the pastor. On one hand I was angry with him but on the other hand, I blamed my sister. Was this idea suggested by her? I knew my sister my whole life and although I loved her, I knew the games she played and the covertness to her actions. I knew my fiancé for only a year but I saw nothing but love, respect and responsibility in him. I chose to forgive him and place most of the blame on my sister and the thoughtlessness of her children. They were good kids who just didn't think about consequences at the time – or maybe they did. To this day, I still don't know the truth of that night in full. The plans were back on, pre-marital counseling was complete but I was not happy with my sister and yet she was my matron-of-honor? My trust in her was severely damaged years before but this made it worse.

Everyone who was anyone in my hometown was there. Over 200 in attendance and it was a beautiful sight. Big fresh magnolia blooms everywhere and candles adorned every corner of the church and reception. As my bridal party was getting ready, I asked my sister to help with my hair; she said no, that she was working on her own. I asked her to please help me steam my dress out and she said no! I asked her to please zip my dress and she said *no!* I said, "You know you are the matron-of-honor and that means you are supposed to help me do some of these things. I'd really appreciate a little bit of help, if you wouldn't mind."

Her reply was, "You're such a self-centered little bitch! You always get what you want but not this time." It took my breath away. It's my wedding day and I'm forced to have you even be close to me on this day, let alone stand up for me what a joke. I thought about how she never really stood up for me and now she is literally "standing up for me!" This idea made me feel sick, as I started to cry. It's my wedding day; thirty minutes before my ceremony begins and I'm crying! Someday she will have to answer to God for things she has done and said.

The ceremony begins as I walk to the back of the church, join arms with my father and he asks me if I'm sure I want to do this. I turned, looked at him and said, "Is it too late to change my mind?" He assured me that it wasn't but I felt it was. So, down the aisle we walked; a walk that I regret to this day... a walk I wish I could not remember!

After the ceremony ended, my new mother-in-law handed me my son and you could hear the whispers as I held my beautiful little baby boy dressed in his little black tuxedo. I didn't care! Say what you want, I thought; I'm happy! Think what you want, draw whatever conclusions you want. I truly didn't care! We hopped in the back of my Dad's '57, fully restored, Chevy and the first thing my new husband said to me was, "I've got you now." Not a good way to start a marriage. He really meant those words too!

The reception was wonderful until my new husband, "John" got drunk and so did his mother. Everything I had grown to know and love for the last year was all changing; in the blink of an eye. All of his groomsmen were drunk and everything that I knew of this man forever changed. It was as if my fiancé had been abducted and this fraud was put in his place. What has happened? This was the beginning of the end. My honeymoon ended the second we said, "I do."

CHAPTER 23

My mother-in-law, "Katie", cared for my son while we went to Hawaii for our honeymoon. The first day was amazing and exciting but when we went to dinner that night he had a mixed drink and made a comment that would haunt me for years to come. He said, "I haven't had one of these for years; since I went to rehab."

What? "Rehab?" I asked.

He proceeded to say that he didn't want to tell me about it before, because he didn't want to lose me, *but* he had gone to rehab twice to kick alcoholism, cocaine and marijuana use. I sat back in my chair feeling like a deer in the headlights. Speechlessly I sat and listened as he went into detail of how his parents spent his inheritance paying for it, but that it worked. He said that he hadn't taken a drink until he went out with my sister's kids, two nights before the wedding. He said not to worry; he can control it, another comment that haunted me throughout our ten year marriage. This started a seven night honeymoon horror story that still leaves me feeling nauseous.

The next morning, my new husband was still in the bar, singing karaoke with some elderly Asian men and I found myself sitting on a bench outside of the bar quietly crying. How could I have not known something like this? What red flags did I miss? Was my mother-in-law trying to tell me this, but couldn't bring herself to jeopardize a good thing in her son's life? Was this going to be the destiny of our honeymoon? I returned to the bar, begged him to leave with me, but he was so intoxicated that he could barely stand so I left and returned to the bench. I cried hysterically and within minutes a man approached and asked me if I was alright. I quickly wiped my eyes; embarrassed to have been seen like that and said, "No."

Well, I was honest. He sat down and asked what he could do to help. I told him everything that had transpired and he arose and went into the bar to try to befriend, "John" and be of some influence. John tried to buy him a drink and got verbally aggressive when the man refused his offer. This nice gentleman returned to the bench and said that. "John" was out of sorts.

You think? He asked me to join him for breakfast at the hotel and I accepted his offer. It was nice to have a stranger that would listen and not have anyone to spread gossip to.

We spent the next week together. He rented a car and we toured the island, ate nice meals, wonderful walks on the beaches, shared open-hearted long talks, watched sunsets and he quickly became a dear friend. He was from London and was there on business. His wife was to have joined him but came down sick with some bug, so she stayed home. She was aware of the situation and was just as lovely as her husband was. Many talks on the phone with her, while her husband was in meetings, forged a friendship between she and I that was just as fast as the one gained with her husband. No, there wasn't anything romantic occurring between he and I; they were both just wonderful new friends. We tracked, "John" down daily only to find him drunk in the bar or passed out in the room. My presence made him angry, as if I was an unwelcome interruption to his process of toxicity. I took the credit card off of the room, so he couldn't build a bar tab but it took me five days to figure that one out. I'd never dealt with anything like this before. I was in uncharted territory.

The last night, "John" wanted to go to a special dinner on the beach. We ate lobster and it turned out that he had gotten a tainted one, which started a new walk through hell. Honeymoon ended but I still exchange Christmas cards with my friends in London every single year. John never knew any of that but always acted surprised when I got a card from England. I tried to talk with him about it many times, only to have him get angry and have a reason to drink. So, I stopped trying to talk to him, our walk consisted of small talk.

CHAPTER 24

Our return from Hawaii, was quickly filled with a reality that I had never known and wasn't prepared for. The tainted lobster resulted in full-blown diverticulitis, surgery, a colostomy bag and 18 months of pain-killers. Moreover, I seem to have gotten "pregnant on the honeymoon" which would have to have taken place in Chicago on our wedding night, but nevertheless, I was pregnant with my second child. I had mixed feelings, in that I was still in shock over the honeymoon, this stranger I call husband, his emergency surgery, returning to a six month old baby and my new husband's craving for alcohol, even his changing a script for pain pills so as to get more... while telling his parents that I did it. A new nightmare had begun!

Eight months pregnant, I had a head-on collision that nearly resulted in early delivery. Diagnosed with toxemia, I found myself hospitalized and relying on my in-laws to care for my son. I returned home, with my son in tow, only to find my husband drinking while on pain pills. He was erratic and aggressive. I tried to phone my in-laws but they weren't home. I could not drive and "John" was raging drunk. I picked up my keys and my son, while he was resting in my carry-all and was going to leave. I didn't feel safe but I was *so* big and *so* sick, let alone feeling weak. He grabbed the carry-all from me, set "Jonathan" down across the room from me, and I began to speak very lovingly and calmly to him. "John, everything is ok. I just need to go get milk for the baby and since I haven't seen him this week, while I was hospitalized, I thought I'd take him with me." He screamed, saying I wasn't going to take him anywhere. He was out of control! He took a gun out of his waistband and began waving it around. Oh dear God, I'd had that gun hidden for years; how did he even know I about it? I scanned the room and realized that I couldn't get to my son. I calmly walked over to "Jonathan", picked him up and walked to the front door. As I was walking out the front door, "John" grabbed the carry-all out of my hands, shoved me out of the house and slammed the door behind me; locking it. I began to beat on the door and screamed; to no avail. I started up the steps to the parking lot, to see if anyone there could help me, but nobody was there. I heard him come out of the front door and say he was going to kill me. I ran and did my best to hide, but he chased me through the parking lot with the gun and I thought I was taking my last steps in life. I was praying for my child within. Please God keep this baby safe and my son in the house. "John" walked up to me, pointed the gun to my eight month pregnant, severely swollen belly and said, "You're lucky I love you." He turned, ran into the house with the gun and I ran after him. I looked through the window and he had placed the gun on the countertop and was sitting in a chair in the kitchen. "Jonathan" was safely sitting in the other room. I had to get to a phone. I began beating on the doors of neighbors, until an elderly black woman let me in. She gave me the phone and I called the police, while hiding underneath her kitchen table. She had her hand on my shoulder and prayed over me. "Please God keep this mother and her children safe. Yes, please God, help us." I heard the sirens and thanked God.

The police arrived, got "John" to open the door and bring the baby to safety. "John" had called his parents and they arrived shortly after the police. I told the officer everything and there were two officers talking to "John." The officers told me that there was no proof of anything, as there were no bruises, cuts, etc. "John" told them that I was being hormonal and he went from acting like a raging lunatic, to a calm, reasonable, well-spoken man. The police bought his story and *nothing was done*! Once again, I couldn't even trust the police to protect me and now they also hadn't protected my children.

Of course, I refused to stay in the home with him, so "Jonathan" and I went to stay with his parents. His parents were angry with him and let him know it. As we were leaving, "John" said to his parents, "You know I'm your son and blood is thicker than water." His mother stopped, turned and looked at him and said, "You're right, son." We left for their home a place of safety, warmth and love, so I thought. Once we arrived, his mother took us to the guest room and got us settled in for the night. I was still crying and as she was leaving, I asked her for a hug. She said, "No, I cannot take your side over my son's." Things between me and my in-laws would never be the same. Interesting how a handful of words can change your path forever.

During the next eighteen months of walking through hell, I gave birth to a beautiful little girl that I named "Lindsay", tried everything possible to get my husband the help he needed, and sought support from his family; all to no avail and I was at the end of my rope. He had financially ruined us and we were on the edge of losing the home I had worked so hard for. He hadn't worked a day during our marriage; not one penny brought into the household by him but he didn't hesitate to spend every dime available. He told me whatever I needed to hear so that I could be his meal ticket through life. He said marrying an educated woman was the smart way to go. Really? Even with a handful of college degrees, I was unable to find employment anywhere, doing anything. I found myself picking up aluminum cans, for milk for the babies and after a three hour stint of doing so, I came home with $6.00 cash, jumped into the shower and by the time I was out, my money was gone and so was "John." He had taken the money and walked to the liquor store for a $5 bottle of booze, instead of milk for the kids. I was done!

I had just completed yet another graduate degree but there wasn't any employment to be found in my area, so I expanded my search. Within two weeks I got a job offer in a tropical state. That was it; the kids and I were going! "John" was informed of my choice and the ultimatum was given. You see, I was brought up with the idea that divorce wasn't an option. His family was told, his drinking buddies were given a permanent invitation to never visit our new life and the house was put on the market. Within two weeks, the house was sold and within a month we were on our way to a *new life*. Wrong! Geographical relocation is never the answer but I was employed and we could eat! The beginning of a walk through hell; while looking at paradise.

CHAPTER 25

Four years pass. I bring in a great living, while helping others change their lives and behind doors my life is a mess. It's true when they say that the plumbers' pipes are always leaky. Shortly after our daughters 3rd birthday, she "fell" out of a second floor window. I thought he had to be involved but "Lindsay" told the doctor that she wanted to "go to heaven to be with Jesus." *What?* "The man named Baxter told me to do it, Mommy." This was the start to a long road of auditory and visual hallucinations, suicide attempts and more.

Our precious little girl was diagnosed with early onset of Childhood Schizo-Affective Disorder with psychotic features. This was so incredibly rare and I genuinely couldn't wrap my brain around it. "Lindsay" suffered, we all did. I remember my mother-in-law telling me, "Physician, heal thyself." My in-laws accused me of not helping my husband and daughter as much as I could. I could clearly see the irony in this one. I went to work every single day helping those struggling with mental health issues and then came home to more. The stress was unbearable. "Lindsay" had been thrown out of 13 daycares before kindergarten and too many babysitters to count; all leaving the house in tears. What was I to do? These years were filled with doctor visits, diagnostic testing, medications, counseling, constant vigilance so as to keep everyone safe and all the while "John" was absent from the home or under the influence of something.

His laziness, alcoholism, verbal abuse, financial abuse, emotional abuse, candy-coated fatherhood, facades, charisma, deception and no financial support or assistance took its toll. Genuinely, not more than $300 total was ever brought into our home, by him, in our whole marriage but he lived well! His parents would come to town and he went from being a drunk, shoving single dollar bills into the g-strings of strippers, to cooking on the grill, playing good father and husband.

I continued dealing with repeat brain tumors but always seemed to get them under control. I begged "John" to attend church with me, go to counseling, even date nights but everything was a "no way". He eventually drank so much alcohol one night, while the children were sleeping over at a church slumber party, that "John" had an alcohol-induced psychotic break, doing over $10,000 damage to our home in less than ten minutes. The police were called and "John" was pepper-sprayed, tackled in the yard, arrested and Baker Acted (in Florida, that's the legal provision for an involuntary mental evaluation). He was diagnosed as mentally ill and life got worse. His family hated me and "John" went wild; using this diagnosis to unleash the hell that resided within him. "John" lived in a place of guilt due to "Lindsay's diagnosis being such a hereditary illness. He suffered too but everything was a reason to drink.

Why was I ignoring and sacrificing my needs and allowing this to continue? Let alone the needs of the children. I had created my own family secrets! What appeared to be perfect, at first glance, was anything but behind closed doors! The answer was clear to me though. I just wanted to be "right" with God. I had to give my marriage every opportunity for change. I adored my children but I hated my life!

I was chatting with my pastor and he asked me to do a Bible study on Ruth and give a presentation to a group of church ladies. I agreed and did so. While preparing for this presentation, I realized what his reasoning for his request was, to help me see that I had become like Ruth, bitter! Me? Bitter? Yes... and he was right. I knew this had to change. How did this happen? Answer: Slowly and through years of enduring abuse. Dear God, please help me be better, not bitter! I began counseling with my pastor and my first "homework" assignment was to do another study from the Bible. Make a list of everything that God expects of a mother and a wife. This was very validating for me and yet revealing. My mother hadn't protected me and now I wasn't protecting my children like I should have. John was never verbally or physically abusive to the kids but by emotionally abusing me, he was also abusing them.

The next assignment was to do the same, only focus on what God expects of a man as a father and husband. Wow. This was *really* interesting and I was fully engrossed because all I wanted to do was do right by my children, do right by me and be right with God. My studies were completed and I presented them to my pastor. He thanked me and then told me to tell my husband that he needed to come to one counseling session with me or he would need to leave the home and life as he knew it would be over. No Way! My pastor is telling me to do this? I was floored but following his wise counsel, I did so. It didn't go over well but guess who showed up? "John".

We met with my pastor the following day and the pastor handed both homework assignments back to me, as if I had already been instructed on what to do. I was confused but he just smiled at me and sat back in his chair. A few moments passed and "John" became verbally agitated. Pastor told him to stay quiet please and "John" shut his mouth and sat back in the chair. It hit me like a steel-toed boot had hit my forehead. The pivotal moment arrived! In a very calm voice I shared with "John" the list of things God expects from a woman as a mother and wife. I asked him if he felt that I had met those aspects... He said, "Yes, hell yes; you're the best wife and best mother I could ever hope for my kids." I thanked him and then proceeded to share what God expects from a man as a father and husband. I asked him if he felt he was meeting those expectations and his reply shocked me. He admittedly said, "Hell no." I asked him if he was willing to get the help he needed, so he could change what needed to be changed? His reply was "Hell no, no way." I asked him if he was sure and he said, "No… why should I?"

Pastor spoke up and said, "Son, this might be your last chance to reconsider."

"John" told him to "f*** off, she'll never leave me because of your God."

Pastor thanked him for coming in and invited him to leave. "John" balked and Pastor told him that he gave up his right to sit in this room with me and told him to leave!

"John" looked shocked but got up and left. Pastor moved closer to me and I was void of emotion; it was all so surreal. Pastor opened his Bible and read 1 Corinthians 7:15 - *ISV – If the unbelieving partner leaves, let him go. In such cases the brother or sister is not under obligation (held accountable); God has called you to live in peace.* I said, "Really?"

Pastor said, "Really!" All I wanted was to be right with God but wait, "John" wasn't leaving; why should he? He had it made. Pastor quickly reminded me of boundary setting and how that was up to me. I was done! My new walk began.

CHAPTER 26

I went and tracked "John" down at a bar. I found him holding hands with some nineteen-year old girl and told him to come with me. The girl told me to mind my own business and I told her to, "Sit down and shut up."

There was a resolve in my voice he had never heard before and I wasn't afraid any longer. We went to the diner next door and ordered coffee. I told him that things were going to change at home and he laughed in my face. I laid out the following: I will no longer cook for you, I will no longer do your laundry, I will no longer clean up after you, I will no longer pay your bills or provide for your lifestyle of shame. The credit card I have in your name is no longer active, I have cleaned out the bank account and have all of the funds in a new bank account. You will go to counseling individually and as a couple, take your medication for mental stability, never take another drink of alcohol, stop with the "titty bars", remain faithful, get a job where money comes into the house fund and spend good quality time with the children. If you don't like it, then you can leave. He said that he refused to do any of it and I said that was fine but life was changing so buckle up; it's going to be a bumpy ride! I was done!

The next two weeks were exactly that but I was resolved and strong! I cooked, cleaned, did laundry and worked but did nothing for "John". He wasn't allowed to sleep in the bed with me, his dirty clothes were piled high, he was always saying he was hungry, his bathroom was disgustingly dirty and he was out of money. Funny but he was home that week more than he had been the previous two years combined. I think he wanted to see if I would follow through but the best part, I put up with nothing from him. I treated him respectfully but he was never respectful in return. When he began to scream or say horrible things to me, I would leave the room. I had to be right with God and do right by the kids, as well as do right by me and I did. Within three weeks, I guess it was too hot, because "John" got a job and found his own apartment.

For two and a half years I had divorce papers waiting in my attorney's office and every three months or so, my attorney would call to see if I wanted to file them yet. I just waited but got a legal separation and that was when the judge told me. "Being a mental health professional, you should be able to handle your husband and even help him." I was livid! Years of hearing these kinds of comments from my in-laws, and now from a judge, in a "No fault" divorce state?

Three years of separation and "John" went off of the deep end. He tried to take out a half a million-dollar life insurance policy on me and then tried to talk two bikers at a bar into "taking me out." When the nurse from the insurance company arrived to take my blood and do the medical exam, I realized something wasn't right! Something clicked in my thinking. She called the agent who quickly came to my home. In the presence of these two, I called "John" to thank him for kindly thinking of me and the kids, and that I understood his thinking and I agreed with him. I should have insurance but that I knew he couldn't afford to keep the policy up, so I told him I would take them on as owner and put the kids as beneficiaries in a trust fund.

He snapped and said that I was, "F-ing with his financial future." The face of the insurance agent lost all color and as soon as we were off of the phone with "John," the agent made some calls of his own. I started the policy with safeguards in place, got a new whole-house alarm system and the craziness got crazier.

Within 30 days of "John" attempting to gain life insurance on me, my home was sold. I took the children and went into hiding and divorce papers were served! The same judge demanded that I give "John" visitation rights to "Lindsay" but I could keep "Jonathan" safe because he wasn't his child and I never allowed "John" to adopt him. Thank God I used good logic at the time of my son's birth.

CHAPTER 27

During this period of time, I met someone who quickly became my best friend. We met in a freak manner, neither one looking for a new friend. We were both in the same place but for different reasons. I was there holding a business meeting and he was there to talk with his son, who had just left for college. Conversations started and led to a beautifully supportive friendship with no secrets, complete honesty and wise counsel. He lived in another state but friendship gapped the miles, thanks to the Internet, phone lines and the fact that I was self-employed and he was newly retired. It's important that I interject Tom at this point. This new friendship was a ray of sunshine and he was a good person. To say the least, I was thankful.

Over months, our friendship grew closer and Tom came to visit. This was the very first time we would see each other face-to-face because we met on line. I know what you're thinking but neither of us were there for romantic reasons and neither of us were open for anything serious. Tom arrived and we had the best time. He was a perfect gentleman, enjoyed the children and they enjoyed him. It was honest, simple and pure friendship. When I took him to the airport, he became tearful and what he said next could have sent me running to or from him but he played his hand wisely. Tom said, "I just really value our friendship." Awww... I did too; everything was great.

The next time we saw each other was when I was in his state for business. He drove to the city, picked me up and we went sightseeing for a couple of days and then back to his house. I met his family and it was a great time of fun, food, new faces and new places. The kids were with a dear friend of mine so I knew they were safe. I couldn't take too much time away so the trip was short, but sweet. When Tom took me to the airport, I became tearful. He asked me what was wrong and I simply replied, "I just really value our friendship!" He smiled, we hugged and I was off to reunite with my beautiful children and get back to work.

My new home and anonymity gave the kids and I a sense of peace and safety we'd never felt before. We had a ton of laughter, joy, great night's sleep, new friends but there were still ties that bind. Lindsay's visitations with "John". I didn't want to keep "Lindsay" from her father and visa versa, but he was unstable and that scared me. I know what he's capable of and her being alone with him, scared me to death. I know he loved her but he was spiraling downward and that meant an unpredictability that I was all too familiar with, yet I had to follow the law!

Tom came to visit the second time and it was during that visit that my life totally went out of control.

CHAPTER 28

Months of visitation led to a pivotal point, which changed the face of our lives and his forever! "John" went to pick "Lindsay" up at school and told the teacher that "Lindsay" wouldn't be coming to school any longer. When the teacher inquired as to why, "John" told her, "because, I'm taking her into the woods, putting her out of her misery and then killing myself."

That teacher was so wise. She didn't show any emotion, said that she understood and then told "John" that she would have to go and get the release form from the office for "Lindsay" to no longer be in school. He agreed, so she reached down and took "Lindsay" by the hand and said, "Come on, honey, let's run to get it together. Okay?"

"Lindsay" left with the teacher and according to court documents, the teacher took her to the front office, called authorities and "Lindsay" was taken into protective custody. Thank God for wise and caring educators!

I was notified by police officials later that evening but we were not allowed to pick "Lindsay" up or even see her, until this was addressed in a court hearing the next morning; Tom and I were there bright and early. I cannot express the panic, fear, sadness, anger and distress in my heart. I cannot fathom what my darling daughter must have thought or felt; if she was aware of her surrounding enough to even comprehend any of it. This was one time that I prayed she was out of touch with reality altogether. Please God keep "Lindsay" safe tonight give her peace; my prayer that rapidly cycled through my thoughts that whole night.

When we arrived to the courthouse, "John" was there, along with a woman I knew and respected. She was a social worker and a friend of "John's" parents. I was so glad to see that there was a voice of reason and sanity sitting alongside him. Supportively, Tom stayed to my side but didn't intervene in any way. I sat down next to "John" and this family friend. I took him by the hand and said, "John, I need you to tell me the honest-to-God's truth! Did you tell Lindsay's teacher that you were going to take her into the woods, kill her and then kill yourself?"

He looked me square in the eyes and with a cold, detached stare, said, "Yes."

I asked him to think again very carefully, and be truthful… he said, "Yes." I asked him why he would say such a thing and he said that he meant it! I couldn't believe what I was hearing and yet I could. I was filled with emotions, which ran the spectrum. On one hand I wanted to kill him and on the other hand, I felt sad for him because he was losing everything he loved. I had gotten to the point where I could separate the person from the illness, but still protect us where and when needed! The law didn't protect us or things would have never gotten to this point! But here we were.

We met before the judge and parameters were laid out before him. How in God's name did this man get this far, with so many brushes with the law and still didn't get locked up is beyond me! Why did "John" do this? Was he trying to get Lindsay the help she needed and getting her into the system would speed that up? She was on every wait list known to man; to no avail or did he say this because he genuinely couldn't live with the sickness of all of it and the guilt that his walk consisted of? I don't know but now the law was going to protect my daughter.

We went through proper channels and in time, yes time, we were granted a permanent restraining order and "John" was never allowed to see or talk to his daughter again. This broke my heart but I had no choice and now neither did he.

"John's" parents blamed me for all of this. I could never do enough but I wasn't God and "John" turned his back on Him and us. They could blame me if that made them feel better; but at this point I didn't care. I tried my best to maintain contact with them so Lindsay had a sense of family in her grandparents but even that was strained after her grandmother broke the restraining order.

"John" had disappeared and nobody knew where he was. His parents denied knowing and he had closed his little detailing and window tinting shop without any forwarding address. Lindsay was talking with her grandmother when all of a sudden, her father gets on the phone and says, "Hi Baby Angel."

She started crying and said, "Daddy? I'm not supposed to talk to you." Conversation over and that was the last time she was ever to hear his voice, something that haunted her for many years.

CHAPTER 29

Tom and I had continued getting closer and it was healthy, pure and wonderful! His last visit rendered some frightful events in life but it seemed to drive us closer than ever. I had never had anyone support me like this. I had his total acceptance, approval, friendship; with no hidden agendas whatsoever. Something shifted during that trip and when I took him to the airport for his return flight, we both cried. It was clear. We both valued our friendship and the changes that were ensuing. If God had let me know ahead of time that he was bringing someone into my life romantically I would have put the brakes on in a serious way but God has his ways.

When Tom returned a month later, it was magical. Three days into his stay, a visitation team came by, to say hello, from the church we went to the Sunday before. Very nice people and the pastor sat down and began talking with Tom, as I was chatting with the other two people. Little did I know then but Tom told the pastor that he loved me and wanted to make sure that he would spend eternity with me in Heaven, so would the pastor please tell him how. Pastor gave Tom Bible verses that explained that we are all sinners and fall short of the glory of God. Jesus was the Son of God, born of a virgin, died on a cross and sacrificed his life for our sins. All he had to do was to believe in these things, pray and ask God to forgive him of his sins, come into his heart and help him live a life that would bring glory to God. Tom did this and with that prayer, we'll spend eternity in Heaven; with all of those who have done the same. I was so happy for Tom because I know the beauty and peace that comes with that knowledge which is there for everyone.

The day before my divorce was final (four years in the waiting), Tom was acting really funny. He had left this leather fanny pack in the car and "Jonathan" picked it up and was carrying it in for Mr. Tom. Tom became panicked when he realized he didn't have it and it wasn't in the car. His mind calmed when he saw "Jonathan" had it and he had the strangest look of relief on his face.

Later that night, he and I were going out for dinner to celebrate the finalization of my divorce. We went to a beautiful beach area just as the sun was beginning to set. Around here it's ritual for people to go watch the sun set, so that's what we did. There weren't many lounges available so we both sat on one. I was closest to the water and Tom was sitting behind me. People were walking down the beach, hand in hand as the sun began to set and it was absolutely beautiful. All of a sudden, people stopped and were looking right at us. What are they doing, I wondered. The sunset is the other direction. As I turned my head to see what they were looking at, I saw Tom on one knee holding a little white leather box, opened and holding the most beautiful solitaire diamond ring in it. My mind wasn't grasping what I was seeing but I sat and listened as he spoke. He told me that he'd been a bachelor for fifteen years and everyone kept asking him why he wasn't remarrying. He said, "I'd always reply by saying that I would when God brought the right woman in my life. Mitzey, I want to spend the rest of my life loving you and your children. Will you do me the honor of spending the rest of your life married to me?" I genuinely didn't see this coming so fast! This was only the fourth time we'd seen each other face to face but I chose to love this man! There was no falling into it it was a choice. He was healthy, loving, independent and strong, everything I had ever wanted in a partner and father for my children and I was in love. Apparently he was too. Of course I said, yes and applause exploded around us. The man was perfect for me. The millennium diamond ring was beautiful (that's what was in his fanny pack). The proposal was amazing and I couldn't be happier. Just as the sun was setting, a new dawn was beginning in our lives and the acceptance was sealed by the sweetest kiss of my life. We celebrated with dinner, went home to talk with the children and everybody was thrilled. I went to my final divorce hearing with an engagement ring on my finger and "John" didn't even show. I had given him every chance and he'd spit them all back in my face. I was done! But he wasn't.

CHAPTER 30

The children were sad about the divorce but excited about getting a new daddy and as Lindsay put it, "a good daddy." Although this made me feel mixed emotions, I could not change the choices "John" had made. This was a new time in life. A time of excitement, newness, love, tenderness, quality time as a family and even gaining new family.

The wedding date was set. Tom and I would be getting married the fifth time we would be seeing each other face-to-face. He had long talks with his son who was in college and his son was happy for his dad; giving him his stamp of approval even if it meant his dad would be moving away. I met his family and they were wonderful, totally loving the children too. Tom was amazing! Things are happening so quickly and yet I have the sweetest peace I'd ever known.

Wedding was approaching and we chose to get married in Tom's hometown, so all of his family could be there. My father agreed to be present, even though he thought I had totally lost my last ounce of sanity. I get it and to outside eyes, I can see that viewpoint. Shortly before the wedding, Lindsay had a setback and needed to be placed in an acute psychiatric facility. Her medicine stopped working and she needed help, which we were unable to provide at home. I was sickened that this had happened right before the wedding. Tom and I discussed everything in detail and decided to follow through with plans as they were set.

The doctors diligently worked with Lindsay the days and weeks prior to the wedding and they agreed that she would be able to do a day trip but nothing longer than 48 hours and nothing out of state. Although that was great; the wedding was out of state and it was too close to change. Tom had a great idea. We decided to do a second wedding locally, so Lindsay could be part of it. He privately chartered a yacht, invited thirty of our local friends, my family (since I knew they wouldn't come) and of course Lindsay. We would do a mock ceremony, the children would give me away and Lindsay would get to wear her beautiful "wedding dress" that matched mine. What an amazing man God had sent my way. I worked things out financially by getting our wedding covered by a local wedding magazine and we were going to be on the cover. Our wedding story touched the editors so much that they dubbed our wedding as "wedding of the millennium". With this coverage, I was able to get vendors to donate their time, products and services for their mention in the magazine. God blessed our efforts and things were falling in place. It was quite a few years before Lindsay ever knew that the "real" ceremony took place a week earlier and in another state.

Tom wanted me to have the wedding(s) that matched our love. My dress was a one-of-a-kind; not by some famous designer but a museum piece that was utterly breath-taking. It had been in a bridal museum which had been closed for some reason and this piece slipped between the cracks. The ridiculous antique beading and pearl appliqués were unbelievable. I designed a train and had it made for the dress. It matched every detail and I am still in awe that we were able to make that happen. Minimal alterations and I drew out my idea of a veil and Tom surprised me by having it special ordered and hand-made. It was cathedral-length with satin-rolled edging and small satin florets, around the full edge of the veil. I cried as I unwrapped and drew it from the large box it was delivered in.

Wedding(s) dates were fast approaching. My father flew in to help "Jonathan" and I transport everything for the desert wedding and off we went. This was to be the "real" wedding. The ceremony was held at a beautiful desert resort, in an old Mexican courtyard, at sunset at the base of the Tucson Catalina Mountains. Every detail was set: formal, delicious food, forty friends of Tom's, my two dearest friends, his family, "Jonathan", my father, tiny details put together with love, a white dove release, harpist and genuine healthy love.

We arrived in Tucson, settled into the hotel and the fun began. Families being joined together with laughter, love, welcoming hugs and joyful hearts. Wedding day had arrived and every detail came together smoothly, without glitch, other than the doves got loose in Tom's house and he, my dad and "Jonathan" couldn't catch them. They all bonded with laughter as they were running through the house, in their tuxedos, trying to catch these birds that thought it was their time to shine and break loose. I still recall thinking how glad I was that one of them didn't choose to nail my gather in his bald spot. He had a history of that after all.

My beautiful attendants and I waited for the ceremony to begin, while waiting in a beautiful formal drawing room. The videographer began asking us questions and when he got to me I just smiled and talked to Tom. I wasn't the least bit nervous and as I spoke to him, via the camera, I told him, "Tom, I love you so much and am honored that you see me as worthy to be loved by you. When I was a little girl, I had a very special hope chest. A cedar chest that didn't look like much because of the abuse it had endured, but it was very special. I filled it with hopes for the future. One of those hopes was that I would someday be worthy of a good, loving man who loved me for who I was, all that I'd been through and saw me as pure, clean and perfect. Thank you for being that man. As you see me walk down the aisle to join you, I pray that you see my clean heart, my pure love and how perfect we are for each other. My hand will slip into yours, our vows will flow from our lips, our rings will slip onto our fingers and our bond will forever be forged. May you love my children as your own and our children merge as brothers and sister. Today, my love, I give you me!"

With those words, the harpist began to play and that was our cue. My attendants began to glide down the aisle and as I came to the gate of the garden, my eyes met my first love "Jonathan". We smiled at each other and his eight-year old little hand reached up and took mine. He looked at me with such love and adoration that my heart soared. He slowly began to guide me into the garden and as he walked me down the aisle to meet Tom, the garden was filled with birds that began to sing all at once, as if we were in some sort of Disney movie. The harpist was playing, hundreds of birds singing, my first love holding my hand and the love of my life waiting at the altar. "Jonathan" gave Tom big hugs and with tears falling from his cheeks, he put my hand into Tom's.

The ceremony was beyond beautiful. "Jonathan" and Tom's son were part of the unity candle ceremony and our families became one. Tears flowed and it was so incredibly beautiful that it drew strangers into the Mexican garden, just to be a part of such a special moment in time.

I am loveable, I am worthy to be loved. My life is worthy to be saved, I am important to many. I am accepted and approved of by all who matter to me. I am doing right by my children, by me. I am right with God.

Many said it wouldn't last. We met in a chat room, engaged after seeing each other four times face to face, our wedding day the 5th time, a horrible damaging childhood, a horrible first marriage. But here we are, over thirteen years later; the children grown and gone, and we're more in love today than we ever thought we could be. Tom, today. I give you me, again!

CHAPTER 31

A new beginning. Tom packs up and within a week moves to join me in Florida so we can start our new life. One week from the day of our wedding, is the second wedding in Florida. We're so excited about it. My father will be there and so will my sister. I was honored that she would be there but grateful that she would not be honored in any other way; like being my Matron-of-Honor. Again, everything went beautifully. Lindsay was doing better and able to be a part of the whole process. It was so special for her! She looked like a seven-year old princess and the yacht was decked out to the fullest. The ceremony was so beautiful that many of our guests didn't even realize that we had gotten officially married the week before in Arizona. We didn't share with everyone because we wanted it to be as authentic for Lindsay as possible. She was lucid and we were so grateful for this. We prayed that she would have memories of this day and they would be dear to her. "Jonathan" walked me down the aisle again but this time walked with a little swagger that made everyone giggle. Lindsay glided down the aisle as if she were royalty. The unity candle ceremony was extra special because she was a part of it and before we knew it, the party was over, the yacht was docked and the magazine was published.

I know that Tom being brought into my life was a reward for handling "John" with grace, love and respect and now we had peace knowing that our new life was calm, safe and loving. I know that I attracted Tom into my life because I was courageous enough to do the work and come to terms with many things from my past, my traumatic issues, my patterns of behavior, my thoughts; both conscious and subconscious. You know, the little voices we hear that remind us of messages we heard in our childhood. Four years of a separation did not happen because I was waiting for this man. It was also so I could come to terms with everything that brought me to that point. I gave myself the gift of time! I took the time, worked hard to understand myself and change and now I was being rewarded. Tom's fifteen-year bachelorhood was also his gift of time, to himself. After his wife left him and their divorce was final, he lovingly injected himself into every aspect of his son's life. He coached soccer, helped with homework, was at every family event on both sides, worked with Michael's mother to assure unity in parenthood and worked on himself. He grew to understand how to be okay with being alone without being lonely and trusted God along the way. He told everyone that he would remarry when God brought the right woman into his life but that he'd never marry a woman with children and he'd never leave Tucson. Well, it's never a good idea to tell God never! I deserved Tom and he deserved me.

This might sound a bit shady and it certainly isn't meant to, however, I've always had this compulsive need to tell Tom's ex-wife, "Thank you." Her choice to cast him aside, without any explanation to him for all of these years, was as if he were trash that was unwanted. One woman's trash is another woman's treasure. I hold no harsh feelings for this woman; quite the opposite. She is kind, gentle, warm and I am grateful. We use the yellow lasagna pan regularly and with each use, I thank God for Robin. Sometimes we think the grass is greener on the other side but only find ourselves standing on Astroturf or in "John's" case, quicksand.

CHAPTER 32

The year 2000 was a year of highs and lows. "John" wasn't finished with us yet. As we celebrated our first Christmas as a family, our first New Year and all that comes with it, there was also a sadness. This was the first Christmas without "John" in their lives. They recalled all of the joys Christmas brought with him in the house; gifts, food, fire in the fireplace, laughter and affection. This was true for them... he usually was able to hold it together for a special day like that but most of what they recalled were things that I had done but put his name on it for them. "Daddy gave you this for Christmas. Daddy made this for you. Daddy wants to read this book to you."; all things that I orchestrated for them. He never bought them a single gift; let alone contribute any money, to purchase gifts. He never offered to read a book to them; I had to push the issue. Regardless, we made it through Christmas and New Years and had a amazing holiday.

It was February, late in the afternoon, when I got a call from a family friend of "John's" parents. It was the same woman who was present the day of the hearing on Lindsay. She asked how we were settling into married life and I assured her we all doing wonderfully. She asked me to sit down, so I did on the edge of the bed. Tom was in the room with me but the children were at school; thank goodness. "Sue" proceeded to tell me that she was sorry to have to call with this news but "John" was living with his parents in Virginia and on Christmas Day "John" was found dead in his bed. What? I couldn't believe what I was hearing but just quietly sat listening; in shock. She went on to say that he'd been in a car accident and had been taking pain killers and as we all know, had a problem with drinking. I started to cry but quietly listened. She said he'd been out with friends the night before, came home and had a long talk with his father, told him how much he loved him and then went to bed. When they went to wake him Christmas morning for breakfast and to unwrap gifts, he was dead. Autopsy report showed an overdose of Hydrocodone. Oh dear God. I began to cry hysterically; I panicked and handed Tom the phone. He finished the phone call and I felt myself running through the house, panicked, as if I was looking for something but really just trying to wrap my brain around it. My first thought was: my love kills. I quickly deleted that thought and then just cried. How was I going to tell the children? How would I explain to them that they would never hear his voice again or feel his hugs? I felt the oddest sense of relief as I felt when my mother died; a relief that suggested that the conflict was completely over. No more head games, no more abuse, no more control, no more feeling useless and unworthy but most of all, no more crazy unpredictability or looking over our shoulders in fear. Why had we not been called before this? It took his parents two months to call us? How was I going to help the children grieve this properly without some sort of funeral etc? I was angry with his parents for not allowing the children to be part of that process but understood with compassion at the same time.

Tom and I sat down to tell the children of "John's" death. We had to do it separately for various reasons which proved to be the right thing to do. Both children surprised me. They didn't cry, they just took in the information and the first thing out of both of their mouths was something about now being safe.

Months and even years since have been filled with tears, multiple "funerals" of our own for him, counseling and Lindsay still looks for her daddy's approval, acceptance, affection in the guys she's dated; a pattern that was a repeat of mine in a strange sort of way. Both children have wonderful relationships with Tom, loving, affectionate, accepting, forgiving, patient and fun. In ways, Tom paid the price for "John's" sins, with the children. They were unable to take it out on "John"… but Tom endured with his steadfast love and dedication; knowing that God brought us all together. I only wish that his relationship with his son, Michael, could have been better. "John" was dead but still not finished with us yet.

CHAPTER 33

Five months after his passing, I started to receive bizarre bills in the mail from creditors that I had never heard of. Magazine subscriptions that were never ordered by me, lines of credit that I had never opened and crazy calls from collection bureaus began. What was going on? I had cleared everything during my divorce so I knew none of this was of my doing. Research got me nowhere except frustrated. I was assured by every supervisor that I spoke with, that everything was done by me. I would know if I had done this… but I was assured. We hired an attorney and the truth began to be revealed. Some of this was "John's" portion of the divorce settlement but the rest of it seemed to be identity fraud. More research showed that my social security number had been used and came from someone at a Virginia residence. Bam… reality hit and "John" had used my social security number to do all of this! After spending a great deal of money on attorney fees, getting some reversed and paying off a few, we were informed that getting this resolved would take many years and lots of money. We were forced into bankruptcy and we were devastated. The "John" walk through hell continued but I was done! We resolved this and let go of it. There wasn't anything to do to fix it and we both just plain wanted all of this to be over.

I kept ongoing communication between the children and "John's" parents and although I always treated them with love and respect, I was continually blamed for his demise. They never shared these thoughts with the children but it was clearly made to me; over and over. I was doing it right and as long as I was doing right by the children, I was right with me and right with God; nothing else mattered. "John's" father Jack was a good man of high standards, values and a kind spirit. His controlling, cold, judgmental and critical mother was a different story, although I never made that known to the children. I felt they would figure things out on their own; in time.

One day, out of the blue, I received a phone call from Jack. He was calm, clear thinking and kind. He told me he had been very ill and wanted to talk to me. I agreed and what I thought would be a courteous ten-minute call; turned into two hours of a private, loving conversation. Jack began to ask for my forgiveness for the way I had been treated. He said that he knew that I wasn't to blame for his son's behavior, choices and death. I began to cry as I listened. He thanked me for all that I did to try to get his son help and for being the best wife I possibly could have been to him. He went on to say that I was also the best possible mother that his he could have ever hoped for; for his grandchildren and he was grateful for that. He thanked me for remaining kind and respectful to he and his wife throughout the years of their bitterness. He told me that he loved me and that he was grateful for Tom in our lives. He shared with me, that the night before "John" had died, they had a long conversation with him and "John" told him that he realized that he had lost everything and everyone that he had loved. He said that he was still in love with me but now I was married to another man and he was unable to even legally see any of us again due to the permanent restraining order. He went on to say that he felt "John" had killed himself as he had hit bottom and it was bad. I told him I appreciated the information but that I felt no guilt because I gave him four years worth of opportunities to get right. He agreed and said that he was glad that I didn't carry any unwarranted guilt. We cried, told each other that we loved each other and I told him not to worry; I had forgive him long ago and I wanted him to feel peace about it all. I prayed with him over the phone, thanked him for the call and his heartfelt apologies and kind words. We hung up the phone and within a week, he died. Two months after he died, his wife ("John's" mother Katie) called to inform us of his death and I wept like a baby. She was shocked by my reaction and when I told her about his call to me. She said that he never told her about the conversation or even about him making the call. This didn't surprise me because he knew that she would discourage his choice. It was a kind call and although she isn't nasty to me any longer, I cannot help but be sad that the children and I couldn't be there to honor him at his passing. This was yet another loss that the children were robbed the chance of proper grieving; all at the hands of their grandmother, more control. Regardless, she's their grandmother. I always make sure that the children called and sent Christmas gifts, cards, flowers and even attempts to visit. She always refuses their pleas to come visit and I'm concerned that someday their requests will cease. When the kids turned eighteen, I no longer bridged the relationship for them. For a while, they didn't make any attempts but over the last year, they are beginning to forge their own relationships with her. Roots and wings! Both aspects must be given.

CHAPTER 34

Tom's son Michael was a fine young man, in heavy pursuit of his undergraduate degree and social life. Tom tried desperately to maintain closeness with him as he grew older but the distance started in high school, the busier he became. Michael was busy with studies, socializing and from what I understand, grew more and more unavailable. When Tom moved to Florida, this continued and the geographical distance just made it worse.

I wanted to move to Arizona so we could be close to Michael, making the new family bonds tighter but we had no choice but to live in Florida. There weren't many resources for children with severe special needs in Arizona at the time but there were unlimited resources in the Sunshine State. Tom moved to Florida and since Michael was fearful of flying, he has yet to come visit.

Over the years, Tom would call, email, text and use every form of communication known to man but get hardly any response from his son. I sent encouragement cards while he was in college but never even got an acknowledgment of receiving them. I continued to send them and gifts from time to time to no avail. I cried as I watched this wonderful man pace the floors on Christmas, Father's Day and other special holidays; just waiting for the phone to ring so he could hear his son's voice but hardly ever a returned call take place. Tom would return to Arizona once or twice each year to see his son, but would find himself holding up in a hotel, waiting to hear back from Michael with his schedule. I chose not to go to Arizona too often, partly because "Lindsay's" needs were so great but also because I knew my husband. He would be concerned to make sure that my needs were met and I didn't want to take away from his time with Michael. I wanted him to be able to focus a hundred percent on his son while he was there. Little did I know that those trips were sometimes lonely trips because he would be waiting with bated breath to see if his son would have time for him. Don't get me wrong. Michael is a great young man but I couldn't figure out the deal with this huge distance in their emotional relationship. I felt guilty as though I had taken his dad away from him but Tom assured me that wasn't it he said it started long before I came into the picture. He reminded me that kids change as they get older and no longer have as much time to spend with their parents. I prayed this would never happen to "Jonathan" and Lindsay but just chose not to worry about the future.

Time passed, holidays passed with very little contact. This fine young man has to feel a sense of abandonment from his dad.

How couldn't he? What can I do to help? What can Tom do? Michael gave him the stamp of approval before he even proposed to me but was he being honest with his dad or just trying to not rock the boat? These are all questions that haunted me for years but Tom was a pillar of strength, never wavering in his belief that Michael was "just too busy." I didn't buy that but had no choice! All I could do was to pray for them both and that's what I did.

Thirteen years went by until Michael got engaged, and I had joined Tom on a trip to Arizona to meet her. We were so proud of Michael. He had accomplished great things professionally and now had found love.

I found it interesting that his chosen path, in many ways, mirrored his father's. We arranged a family dinner, which would allow everyone to meet one another. She was a lovely young woman with two beautiful small children from a prior marriage. They were obviously in love and we both remembered the look, smiling as we exchanged glances that spoke those words silent words. We looked forward to spending more time with them throughout the next week and getting to know her and I felt so much joy knowing that Tom would be spending good time with his son. Days passed with no contact from Michael. I watched Tom sitting in the hotel, wringing his hands with nervousness and he waited for the phone to ring. His son was "busy" again. My heart hurt for him so deeply but there wasn't anything I could say. I felt angry, sad, protective and outraged. There is no excuse for this and it's just plain rude but I did my best to keep my mouth shut. I know this young man was hurting but I was angry. I was angry at myself for not knowing what hell my husband had quietly gone through over the years, with each visit he took to Arizona and I wasn't there with him. My heart had been in the right place but that was a mute point to me.

I put my foot down, verbally aired my disapproval and told him to not take this! Don't accept this! Force the issue, it's obvious that he's holding feelings that are unresolved and if he's just too "busy" Tom, then he's being just plain rude. So I said, "Straighten him out." Tom reluctantly agreed, made a "demanding" (for Tom it was demanding) call and within 48 hours, breakfast for two was scheduled. This wasn't a time for my presence and I was right.

Tom met with his son, pointblank asked him emotionally difficult questions and without saying a word, the look on his son's face said it all. Hearts had opened, hard shells were cracked and the healing began. There wasn't another minute with his son and future wife during that trip but it was the beginning.

CHAPTER 35

Two months later, Tom got the call that his little brother was getting married to the love of his life, but he knew that he wouldn't be able to attend because we had just visited. It was Christmas 2012 and money was tight due to my taking four months off of work to walk through Europe but it was my chance to give back to my husband. I went upstairs to the office and bought Tom a plane ticket, rented a car and paid for his hotel. This was my Christmas gift to me! Yes, to me. The best gift that I could have ever received was the gift of Tom seeing his brother's face as he walked in right before the ceremony began. My gift to me was the joy of my husbands' tears of gratitude. I wouldn't be able to go with him but I was there in spirit for sure.

Tom surprised his brother on his wedding day and ending up being the only family member present since this "secret" wedding hadn't been announced to everyone else. They were all going to attend a Christmas dinner later that day, which was really the reception. Tom arrived, got lost on the desert road leading to his brother's house, called his brother and two minutes later, they were hugging each other in the middle of a dirt road in the middle of nowhere! Little did Tom know that his brother left the house without telling anyone, so when the pastor passed him leaving the house, he and the bride thought there was a "runaway groom" on their hands. Tom and his brother returned to the house and Tom ended up standing up for his brother during his wedding; giving joy is not just a gift to the person receiving it but also to the person gave it. Love, joy, happiness abound and another love story comes to fruition.

Little did I know that this gift would prove to be so much more. This trip was extra special in that Tom was able to spend six special hours with his son, Michael, his fiancé and her two children. They ate, talked in great depth, laughed, hugs and played together. Tom was present as the children opened all of the Christmas presents we had shipped to them previously and more healing took place. A selfless gift turned into the gift of healing!

Tom and Michael communicate regularly now and do so with love, open sharing and honesty. Two grown men, father and son bridging the gap even though thousands of miles are between them. We look forward to attending their wedding next month and "Jonathan" and Lindsay will even be there. Yet another love story begins.

"Jonathan" is now 22 and lives in Germany; working as a Professor of English with the German government. Lindsay is

21, stable, healthy, loving, God-centered, living independently and able to have in-depth philosophical discussions about life. She's had no breach of reality for several years. I am so honored to have been chosen to be their mother and our relationships are closer than ever.

Our unified family grows closer with each contact and now it's expanding. We embrace these children, our new soon-to-be daughter-in- law, her children and all that comes with them. We look forward to many years of love, laughter, joy and good family time. Life is changing and who knows how long the miles between us will remain.

To this day, I have zero contact with my brother and next to nothing with my sister. I no longer allow people in my life that are abusive and cut me down to elevate themselves. My estrangement isn't out of a spirit of bitterness or un-forgiveness but out of a place of healthy love… self love!

CHAPTER 36

I continue to love myself and love others, walking the walk instead of just talking but I found myself in a business that was built on loving one another but vicious covert people were still present.

As you will soon begin reading about the pilgrims walking, on the Camino de Santiago, I firmly believe that we are all pilgrims walking the Camino of life. There are many types of pilgrims walking through life and one of those types are the competitive jealous ones. They are the pilgrims who are always competing with others; keeping up with the "Jones'", elevating themselves by cutting you and your efforts down. Many people get caught up in this and try to compete back but I got to a point where I stopped letting people know what I was doing no talk… JUST WALK.

My walk in business was one of success and abundance and this made a couple of competitive people very jealous; the covert undermining behavior began. Those following my leadership began to mistrust me and I couldn't figure out why. It took me three years to finally figure out what was going on and heartfelt attempts to appeal to this person, just made things worse. Six years of a conveyor belt of walking on eggshells, damage control and appealing to my "boss" for assistance and resolution got me nothing. My "boss" and I were friends; I trusted her but it became clear over time. I wasn't being protected! I wasn't worthy in her eyes to even protect me. I quickly saw a pattern re-emerging that had to be stopped. Patterns like: manipulating others for monetary gain, using God to gain your own personal pleasure, jealousy, competitiveness, not protecting me and mine and lastly, victimization. I refused to be a victim but I couldn't quite stop the cycle fast enough. I was making big money and we needed the income to help with Lindsay's medical needs and I had many other people relying on my leadership for their own success. Appeals for help resulted in being "smoothed over," issues swept under the rug and things got worse.

Interesting how childhood patterns can be repeated even in a professional nature! This was crazy but it was true. The stress of dealing with this for many years started to make me sick. One illness after another, more brain tumors, complications, on and on until I had enough but how do I change this? Women can be funny creatures but women who are angry can be vicious.

Two experiences with the same patterns, flick my light switch on and the ugliness that had been in the dark, was now illuminated for cerebral change! My thought revival was on and it was time for a revolution of the mind! Life as I'd known it for six or seven years was about to change, my thinking was about to change, my choices were about to change. I was changing again!

CHAPTER 37

Right around the end of this journey, I was asked to be the Matron-of-Honor for my dearest friend's wedding. She was almost like a daughter to me; not just a friend so, I not only joyfully accepted, we purchased her wedding dress for her, I spent untold hours upon hours helping her plan, I did all of her flowers for the wedding and gave her the most beautiful bridal shower one could ever ask for. My generosity in time, talent and treasure couldn't be matched by anyone. She had asked another friend from childhood to be her bridesmaid. This girl was angry that she wasn't to be the Matron-of-Honor and proceeded to unleash an assault on me that was absurd and childish to say the least. I was patient and even offered to step down so as to make things easier for the bride; which was refused by friend. It made sense though. This girl wasn't local, had no money and according to my friend was very self-centered. I couldn't tell you if that were true because I had never met the girl but trusted my friend; mistake.

I refuse to give this bridesmaid many more lines within this book, other than saying that she attempted to ruin the shower by calling me names and having a horrific attitude and this continued through til the end of the wedding. Why did the friendship end? Not because of this ill-behaved young woman but because my friend of seven years didn't stand up for me. She didn't protect me, allowed this girl to hurt me and then justified her silence by talking poorly about me to others. The day of the wedding, the bride went off to the salon, with her friend and I was to go to the venue to do all of the flowers. I joyfully did this because my doing the flowers was a gift to the bride, required fresh timing and I wanted to make sure it was perfect. The bride and my help didn't arrive for hours and I was stuck at the venue trying to sort out the mess made by the caterers and those who brought supplies and just dumped them. So many details, no help other than the groom, his brother and best man who worked on hanging lanterns throughout the garden; I was left holding the bag. It was a mess and I was alone to do everything else. She wasn't answering calls and I was just supposed to be doing flowers. What a nightmare! She eventually showed up with her bridesmaid and helper but I was severely stressed, not feeling well and having to field too many errors made by other vendors. By the time the bride and her help got there; just a couple of hours before the wedding was set to begin, I was fried.

It turned out beautifully but according to the bride, it was the worst day of her life. Every bit that I, my daughter and my husband did that day was with pure hearts and pure love.

We were inseparably close for years but she allowed the influence of covert competitive people to undermine our relationship but most of all, she didn't protect me or stand up for me. The sad part is, my friend knew what it was like to not be protected by someone that she trusted. Why did this happen? Had she just used me to help get her wedding done? Was she another "John" who saw me as a meal ticket to make life easier? I'd spent seven years proving my love, trustworthiness and did nothing but pour into her just to have her allow this? I had people tell me that once she was done with me, she'd drop me like a bad habit but I didn't believe this and still can't. I think she got caught in their webs of manipulation and deceit as I had and just didn't know how to get out of it. I've forgiven these people, and the bride too, but no longer allow them to walk alongside me. *Sometimes, the silence from our friends is far more painful than the vicious words from our enemies.*

The same patterns were present in my childhood, my sister and mother, in business and in friendships! These patterns were once broken but raised their ugly heads destined for repetition. The same messages were ringing through. Money was evil, not good enough, not worthy, accepted or approved of, not important, unwanted and unworthy of being protected.

Forgiveness is the fragrance that the violet sheds upon the heel that just crushed it." – *Mark Twain*. "Sometimes those who wear the prettiest shoes possess the heels that cause the most fragrance." – *Michelle Boss*

I felt no anger towards my friend or my business leader. I felt sad and found myself grieving for their loss as I did for the loss of my mother. Grieving the loss of what should've been, what could've been but coming to a place of fully accepting that it was... what it was!

One cannot lead where they are unwilling to go.

One cannot lead until they learn how to follow.

One cannot be truly served until they truly learn how to serve.

It's time for a thought revival! And I was on my way to yet another walk in life. Unplug or crash. I made my decision; **_unplug_** but how?

PART 4

BIG TALK

CHAPTER 38

I had drawn a line in the sand of my life! I was going to un-plug, detach from daily stressors and people that caused it. I found myself surrounded, socially and professionally, with people who "talked God, love and integrity" all over the place – to everyone – but their lives clearly were lives that weren't "walked with God, love and integrity." Leaders and workers in the Church were butt-covering, narcissistic, self-serving, prideful, excuse making, judgmental, critical and unloving. Professionally, leaders who talked God in a successful manner which manipulated others to do more – to line their pockets – and appear to appeal to those that genuinely wanted to make a difference. Yet if you weren't producing, you were ignored. Sometimes people weren't producing due to needing encouragement. Not everyone is an attention whore. People who talked "professional family" but were as dysfunctional as my DNA family, and instead of protecting me, swept horrible behavior under the rug and smoothed over to keep the appearance of things perfect. Personally, as flawed as I am, I have always tried to "WALK GOD" so others would come to know God. Yet I found my closest circles filled with users, abusers, takers, narcissistic self-serving people that sucked me dry, while feeding me lines of appreciation and admiration, just to keep me alive so as to feed further. All the while, "TALKING GOD". Years of abuse witnessed and felt, personally and professionally. I had lost faith, not in God but in God's people, humanity in general. God didn't cause religious division, war, economic distress, global ecological distress and collapse, people did! God hasn't forsaken his people; his people had forsaken Him. What happened to kindness without expectation? What happened to people who dedicated their lives to selflessly serve God? Serving humbly and joyfully without ego, price, judgment, criticism or concern for "their" ministry. My heart was aching! The only people I had in my life who wasn't like this was my husband, Tom and the two children. I was more than grateful for them but it was the rest of my circle that sucked me dry, making me literally sick.

The first thing I did was to re-evaluate my circle. I began having conversations with "friends" and let them know that I was changing my life and have made drastic choices for change. I made it clear to them that I was getting healthy in every area of my life and that I was no longer going to allow anyone to be a part of my life who didn't invest in me as much as I was investing in them. So, they can either be a part of my life or not. I was okay with whatever their choice would be but that I would only be investing in those who chose to step up to the plate. Within days, my life began to change. I stopped getting calls from people who needed "help" or an "ear" but were never there for me. Why? Because they weren't willing to reciprocate and those days were over. I deserve and am worthy of respectful reciprocation; we all are and yet I was just giving and giving and giving; getting nothing in return! It was even worse than that. The ones who demanded and took the most, were the ones who complained the most and I couldn't seem to give enough to! There were people I had employed for years who would come to work and the first two hours of the paid work day; nearly every day, was filled with tears and problem-solving for their personal lives, many hours lovingly dedicated to some project in their life. Yet nothing much was ever given back to me unless it was on the clock. I loved them, so I gave! Why was that okay for so long? Not any longer! I was tired of the unhealthy messages I was getting from this and the childhood tapes just kept being validated by my adult choices! I was sending myself a new message and that message was. You are worthy of love, respect and meeting your needs.

Over the next few weeks, many tested this new line of thinking by continuing their demands and requests; to no avail. Stress levels began to drop. I stopped saying yes to everything and began to carefully choose because my time and me are valuable commodities. I realized that my not being protected by the leaders of my business was actually affecting my success level in business and I could no longer recruit people to be a part of a group that was "toxic." I felt that I was asking people to trust me and then leading them into the lion's den. I decided it was time to walk. So I did!

My health was eroding and my mortality was staring me in the face. Life had taken a toll on me and I had to un-plug or crash; so I was un-plugging and regaining my footing for my walk through the rest of my life. How and what do I need to do to prepare for this? How and where would I do this? I knew that once I got my health back in every area of my life, I would re-emerge with a new healthy circle of influence, regain success at an all time high and be a better wife and mother than ever. Now was the time, I had chosen health over wealth, over appearances, over public opinion, over status, over social limitations and self-imposed imitations! I was on a mission to *walk* the *talk*...

The Camino de Santiago, being a highly held Christian pilgrimage for thousands of years – I heard one would see God in the pilgrims and those who dedicated their lives to working with the pilgrims. I read all about it through a mandated reading assignment in college. I was 21 years old and I never forgot about what I read. I decided then that someday I wanted to do this walk but life took over. One degree led to another, which led to a handful, two children and so forth. The dream never left my heart. I made my decision and I was going to give myself three months sabbatical in order to finish the 800km/500+ miles treacherous walk. After all, I'm an obese, unfit, middle-aged woman and have a brain tumor. I was going to need all three months if not more. Tom believed in me and that's all I needed; I was going to ride on his belief. He bought me a one-way plane ticket to Paris and two guidebooks so he could follow my journey. He wanted to go but he was unable to take the time off from work. I was going alone. Besides, I think Tom's Camino walk is on a nice cruise ship; just sayin'. This was uncharted territory for me because the only backpacking or hiking I'd ever done was when I was 16 years old; since then I'd only hiked to and from the fridge! My ticket was bought as was the guide book. Now it was time to prepare for this walk to be remembered!

CHAPTER 39

"Jonathan" was living in Germany by this time and then there was Lindsay. Although she was stabilized, I was concerned for her. I wanted this to be an opportunity for her growth, felt the need to have her close and with family. Tom; having to work so many hours on a special project, made it next to impossible to give her the attention and guidance she needed. So, "Jonathan" asked if Lindsay could come and live with him for the summer in Germany. What a great idea! He was responsible, working part time, involved in missions and they had a great relationship; in spite of the difficulties having a sister with special needs brings about. Thank you "Jonathan." Without your bravery and responsible person, I could have never accomplished what you knew that I could. I will never forget what you did for me; you gave me peace of mind during my journey.

The plan was set! We were all three going to meet in Paris for a week of fun and adventure, before I left for the Camino.

We purchased "Lindsay's" one-way airfare and planning ensued. The excitement was magical.

I talked big and I got some sly comments from some people, eye rolls from others, giggles from more and support from others! I found this frustrating and frankly de-motivating, so I shut my mouth! I decided to do no more talking about it. I was going to walk it and they'd see. Who did I think I was? Taking on something like this and doing it with such confidence. I wasn't afraid, nervous, wavering, doubting that I would do this but it appears many were. I didn't care! I was done with what others thought. I was taking my power back and changing my life! I had to heal myself. "Physician, heal thyself." Thank you "Katie," I will! What makes me think I could ever author a book? But here I am, doing it! I hope you have a thought revival; a revolution of your mind! You can do anything you want to do! *A better world begins with the shifting of one man's thinking! Let it be yours!*

CHAPTER 40

Weeks leading up to my departure were filled with magic. I stopped talking about it but nearly each day I came home with a bag of some sort, placed it in the guest bedroom and shut the door. Life for everyone else continued but quietly and secretively my planning ensued. Lists upon lists, research, and more lists! Things were coming together. Hotels for Paris were booked, I took on extra work to put away the funds without it effecting our household budget and I would be borrowing "Jonathan's" backpack that he used to first tour Europe with. I stocked up on three month's worth of canned goods, frozen meats, medications, cat food, litter and everything else I could think of. I wanted to leave the house clean, every possible need of Tom's met in advance and all laundry done! I wanted this to have the least amount of negative impact on the love of my life as possible and I was organized! I had downloaded an audio Bible onto my Ipad, bought a new camera with all of the accessories that were needed to be able to download to the Ipad and update

Facebook. I was unplugging except for Tom and the children. I wanted to make sure that I posted every picture that I took, kept an online and handwritten journal and was able to skype with them as often as possible. You might be thinking that this plan wasn't really unplugging but if you knew how incredibly over-committed and busy I have been, this plan was complete seclusion in comparison. If Tom and the children weren't able to be on this journey with me, then they were going to get the next best thing to it. It never occurred to me that these posts would create such a vast following of people!

Lindsay was preparing for the journey also. She bought some new clothes, moved out of her apartment, put everything into storage and began staying with a girlfriend. She was sticking money away and getting really excited. This was going to be an adventure for her too and I hadn't even really been thinking about that. With each day that passed, the excitement grew.

I made the decision to walk away from my career and the people I was bound to. The minute I did that, what felt like a million pounds of bricks lifted from my chest. This made it real to me! My thinking had changed, messages I was sending to myself had changed, decisions were made and actions were taken. I felt no fear; just excitement and pure unadulterated relief. I will never again allow anyone to have that much power over me. Don't get me wrong, the idea of walking away petrified me for six years leading up to this point but by this time, I was done! Interestingly enough my walk had already began!

We are all walking through life. We take different paths, get distracted, take the wrong path from time to time, sight see, run, slowly smell the roses along the way and so forth but we are all walking a journey. Forget the Joneses you don't need to keep up with anybody, it's your walk! It doesn't matter what color or type of car that you drive, what kind of house you live in, how many zeros are at the end of your paycheck, who you know and what title you have. At the end of your life what will people remember you as? What will your legacy be? Only you can answer that question but for me? I want to please God; not Man. I want to serve God by being of service to Man. I want to love others as God loves us. I want to be a walking example of His love; not for my glory but for His. I want God to work through me and use me up! It's time to un-plug to all of this and plug back into Him, nature and me!

Time to pack. It seemed like a never-ending process of organizing and packing. Once it was over, I nuzzled with Tom as he prayed for my safety and health. I prayed for him and we were off to sleep. Early the next morning we picked up Lindsay and headed for the airport. Okay, we have too many suitcases, can barely get them into my convertible and they are way too heavy. I knew that mine would be overweight but girl, what are you thinkin'? All we could do was laugh and pay the little "token" price that the airline was charging. Wow; didn't I just say that it was time to unload and unplug? Little did I know that all of those clothes that I was taking would never be worn and by the time I was finished with my walk, they would be way too big and fall off of me! Dangit, I could have bought a whole new wardrobe with that "token" I paid for that extra baggage. Sorry, just thinking out loud.

There were hugs, kisses, tears, excitement and waves as we watched Tom pull away from the terminal. Passports in hand, all of the overstuffed, oversized luggage in tow and two excited young girls (give me some slack here) entered the terminal, checked our luggage and made our way to the gate. I remember turning around toward home and blowing a kiss to all of those naysayers who said I'd never even board the plane. These are the same people who are still stuck in their miserable lives, giving everyone else their power and spending their days complaining but taking no action. I lowered my head, said a quick prayer for them and boarded the plane. Paris, here we come!

CHAPTER 41

The flight to Paris was long and the guy sitting next to me had gas the whole way! What in God's name did you eat, brother? It smelled like decomposing flesh and I was beginning to be concerned for the health and well-being of those sitting around him; Me! Lindsay slept most of the way, although I will never know how.

We arrived at Charles De Gaul Airport and within an hour we had all of our luggage and heard our names being called. Up walks this fine specimen of a young man, with a beard! "Jonathan." We all started screaming and running for hugs. I'm sure we gave the French a bad impression of Americans that day. We were laughing, crying, yelling with excitement and hugging to no end. "Jonathan" looked like a tourist with a huge hiking backpack and two other backpacks jury rigged to his body. Struggling to walk with each step and looking like Picasso with the beard, it was too much to bear.

My French sounded more like Russian so obtaining transportation to our hotel was a hoot but "Jonathan" had picked some up so between the two of us, we got there. We checked into our adorable apartment for the week and immediately went for food. We were in Paris. And your question is?

We spent the next week riding the Metro and seeing every site there was to see. We went to the top of the Eiffel Tower and L'Arc de Triomphe, walked the Champs Elysses and even found the store that I purchased my Paris Original dress in when I was 16. We had lunches in outdoor cafes, attached locks with our family name onto the bridge near Notre Dame and on and on. We laughed, were creeped out in the Paris Catacombs and did a jig video in front of Moulin Rouge, for Tom. We were sore from all of the walking but this was great training for my walk.

What an amazing week of building memories but it was the night before I was to leave for the Camino de Santiago and that meant it was time to pack and prepare; yet again. All of my tourist clothing and such was being packed in suitcases and sent to Germany with "Jonathan" and Lindsay. They would be leaving Paris the same day as I was but taking a train in the opposite direction than me.

I started preparing for my walk by asking Lindsay to please cut all of my nails off. She couldn't believe I was doing that since I had been so fanatical about them for so many years but it was time for change and there was no room for frivolity. She cut them and cried. As I packed my backpack with all of the emergency, medical and trekking gear, Lindsay said that she just couldn't believe that I was going to follow through with this. I reminded her that I am a woman of my word and when I say I'm going to do something, it's done! She agreed but said "Mom you always told us stories of your adventures like jumping out of planes skydiving but we've never seen you do anything like that/" I laughed and told her it's because I was raising them and took no chances by the time they came along. She understood and asked why I was taking chances now. There's a difference between reckless risk-taking and taking calculated risks. We talked about my careful research and planning and she got it! She kissed me and headed off to bed. "Jonathan" stayed up with me as I finished packing. I went to lift my backpack and couldn't. We laughed and he hoisted it to my back. I have the picture of me in my nightgown, trying the backpack on for size.

The sun arose and so did I. After strolling the streets of Paris for seven days; completely surrounded by sidewalk cafés, accordion players, street artists, glass ceiling river boats and those in love – I lifted my forty seven pound backpack, dressed for the hike of my life. Lindsay wasn't interested in going to see me off at the train station; I think it was too early for her. She woke to kiss me goodbye and say a prayer together and with that, "Jonathan" and I were off to meet my train. We walked ½ mile to the train station with "Jonathan" holding up my backpack for part of the way. Whew, I came prepared but the weight took my breath away with each step I took. It was so heavy and I prayed that I wouldn't tip over in front of everyone. We laughed, hugged, kissed, took a picture of us together and he asked me if I was sure I wanted to do this. He said, "Let's just take a train to Germany Ma and hang out with me for the summer." How did I get so fortunate to be chosen as mother to these amazing young people. We said a prayer together; I was more concerned for him spending the summer alone with Lindsay, than I was for my own safety but I chose to not verbalize that concern at that time. I boarded my train and I was off.

PART 5

BIG WALK

CHAPTER 42

I was headed to St. Jean Pied du Port France, which was the starting point I selected for my Camino journey, part of the French Route. It was going to be a six hour train ride with a two hour connector in Bayonne, France. I purchased the last remaining seat on the train and was grateful to get it, until I saw what it was. I found myself between cars, sitting in a fold down jump seat that provided support for one butt cheek, no A/C and crying babies that were crying in Hungarian, I think. Is that possible? I laughed, joyfully shed my gear and was beyond thrilled to be sitting in this seat, on the way to a walk of a lifetime. My eyes fed on the French countryside as we passed and I didn't give a thought about what was to come. I just stayed in the moment; soaking it all in, oblivious to the noise and just kept thanking God for the blessings I was experiencing. I felt peaceful, excited, joyful and nervous. By nature I'm a participator that closely observes others and my surroundings along the way. This became an interesting part of my first day's journey, people from every country imaginable; speaking languages that I couldn't even decipher what it was and behaviors that were just as foreign as the language they spoke.

After several hours, we approached Bayonne and it was time to change trains. The whole train idea was new to me; throw French signage into the mix, I was lost *but* one foot in front of the other, using my brain and keen sense of observation, I found myself on the right train! When all else failed, follow all of the backpackers. First lesson learned! Not the stragglers but the large volume of people that are moving in one direction.

The train was filled with eighteen backpackers headed for the Camino de Santiago in St Jean. My second lesson was gained at this time. It became clear that personality differences were going to be an interesting element to this walk. Walkers were called pilgrims during the entire journey on the Camino and I quickly realized from listening to conversations, that there are going to be many "types" of pilgrims. There are those that have walked this journey before and they "know it all; follow me" or the competitive pilgrims who pumped others to find out what their time span for walking the length would be. Then there's the pilgrims that were on it for the "adventure" just wanting fun with no soul-searching involved, or the pilgrims hoping to be healed from cancer or some other life-threatening disease. Very interestingly, they were all chattering in their languages but it was evident what the conversations held, as guidebooks were taken out, maps, iPhones and such. I was the only English-speaking person on board so I just sat and observed. I didn't come here to make friends or socialize, not that I was beyond that or not open to it; it just wasn't my reason. I immersed myself back into the countryside and stayed grateful.

More beautiful sights pass by my window and the scenery begins to change. The mountains are beginning to peek into the horizon and there are creeks and waterfalls everywhere. It's June 23rd, so everything is green and fresh, in full bloom. Breathtaking beauty surrounded me, from the mountains, to the flower boxes overflowing with bright colorful cascading flowers, the gushing waterfalls, cobblestone roads, sheep grazing in lush green pastures and amazing architecture. The train slows down and we see the train depot ahead for St Jean Pied De Port. The tension and excitement grows amongst the backpackers. With everyone scrambling to grab gear, one could begin to see personalities emerge again. Some pilgrims would lend a helping hand to others and some just pushed their way through the same pilgrims they were sharing their plans with just a few moments prior. This is going to be interesting, to say the least.

I lifted my 47 pound backpack and carefully hoisted it upon my already sore shoulders. I remember waiting to be the last off of the train and praying that nobody would see me struggle with it! Dear God, please don't let me tip over from the weight of this backpack and if I do, don't let anyone see it happen. Laughing at hearing myself praying this nearly audible prayer of vanity, I grabbed the straps, locked myself into that bad boy and stepped off of the train. I was greeted by a beautiful sign that said Welcome to St. Jean Pied de Port and there was my first arrow. WOW; my first arrow. You see on the Camino, pilgrims are guided along the journey by arrows, painted on the sides of barns or rocks formed together to make an arrow. They come in *all* types and colors so the pilgrim must be diligent in two things: keeping their eyes open for them *and* trusting them. Third lesson learned and one that would prove to be growth-provoking during this journey. You see, hundreds of thousands have gone before me and marked the way; I needed to trust them and my trust was bankrupt. Lessons that helped and haunted me throughout the next three months of my life, and I continue to see parallels in many areas of my life since.

CHAPTER 43

As I left the train depot, I began to walk to the center of town. As I passed beautiful homes with huge flower boxes and gorgeous architecture, I felt this sense of peace come over me. I was anonymous here! Nobody knew my name, knew my history, demanded anything from me, needed me or even cared what I said or did. I didn't have a cell phone, email, car, bills, responsibilities other than for myself and my job was to just put one foot in front of the other and walk! I decided that I wanted to not just walk but to **WALK THE TALK**; letting others **SEE** God in me after all, it all has to start with me. If that's what I'm looking for, then it starts with me!

The town center is lovely. Ancient, cobblestone streets, narrow steep walkways curbed by beautiful buildings and narrow doors! I am looking for the Official Camino Pilgrim Passport office but keep getting distracted by the charming surroundings. I found it as evidenced by the line of backpacking pilgrims waiting at the entrance.

In this office I would register as a pilgrim and obtain my "Credencial del Peregrino" or my Pilgrim Passport for the Camino de Santiago; also called "The Way of St. James". This journey is a spiritual pilgrimage that winds through all types of terrain within Europe but all roads and paths lead to Santiago, Spain, where the remains of St James the Apostles' remains are said to be buried in the Cathedral called Santiago de Compostela. From St Jean to Santiago is approximately 800 km or 500+ miles of walking. I am so incredibly excited as I await my turn. As I approach the desk, a German man with blondish hair and full beard greets me and we sit down. This is so official. I pay my fee for the passport and I am given this accordion looking booklet. He proceeds to explain to me that every night I must get the booklet stamped from where I am staying, best having 2-3 stamps in it per day. Each bar, restaurant, hotel, pension', hostel or albergue' has their own unique stamp. When I complete the journey in Santiago and show proof that I walked the whole way, book filled with stamps showing my journey's path, I will receive my "Official Compostella" from the powers that be! I will also be allowed to participate in the Pilgrims' High Mass in the cathedral. I shut off the childhood tapes that were running in my head, signed my document and committed to completion, getting my very first stamp. I was doing this for me because I deserved a win, a victory, a change, a healthy life and it was my time; I made the time. After pictures were taken and the German man grabbing three or four kisses on my cheek, I left the office on a new high. Why would anyone choose drugs or alcohol when there are highs like this? My mind darted to "John" for a split second and then I left all thoughts of him sitting in that pastor's office and that is where they continue to stay to this day.

I had made reservations for this quaint little hotel in the center of town. I knew ahead of time that the accommodations along the journey would be primitive at best so I saw this as my last chance to experience luxury, a great night's sleep and maybe even shave my legs. I laughed at the thought of vividly picturing my leg hairs braided as I hobbled into Santiago. The whole night I had this strange sense of deja vu, even in the hotel room I kept brushing it off as fatigue. Dinner time was fast approaching.

Grabbed by a fast talking, high energy New Yorker and begged to join him for dinner, I ended up with four other pilgrims who joined our table and an evening filled with observation. I didn't want to have dinner with anyone and certainly not a hyperactive person. I was there for peace and detachment. Why did I agree? Once again, not listening to my needs, I buckled but it was all part of the plan. By the evening's end, there were twelve of us at the table, pilgrims from Korea, US, Germany, Belgium, Kuwait, Iran, Ireland, Australia and Italy. Everyone shared their "why" and their plan of attacking the journey. I just smiled and sat with a listening ear as the competition began but didn't share my real whys or my plan… I would have been embarrassed to share that, in fact, I had no plan other than to just put one foot in front of the other. I remember a quote I heard at one point in my life that said a journey of a million miles starts with the first step; that was my plan. I hadn't thought about the second step!

CHAPTER 44

I awoke after a good night's sleep, and began to prepare for my first day on the Camino de Santiago. Having a giggle resounding in my head over last night's dinner companions, I entered the bathroom to take a shower and I heard myself say, "Oh my Gosh". I was looking at the shower and the door to the shower was as tiny as tiny could be! Didn't Europe have any clean fat girls? I couldn't believe I wasn't going to be able to shower because I couldn't get my fat butt through the shower door! I was in shock and then I got angry! Sucking in every body part possible, I squeezed my obese body through the door opening and felt like I just came through the birth canal, as I emerged on the other side. I was pleased with myself but decided right there and then that I was done with being fat! This fat girl, was in Europe, clean with cleanly shaven legs to boot. Don't ask me how that was accomplished; many miracles took place and this was the first.

As I was dressing and packing my bags, I noticed a small plaque on the wall, stating that the room I was staying in was the same room used in an American-made movie about the Camino. A very famous actor had stayed in this room during the movie and it was in some of the movie shots too. That's why I've had this strange sense of dejavu; I saw the movie shortly before departing for Europe and it was still fresh in my mind.

I gathered my gear, laced up my boots, said a prayer and headed for a pilgrim's mass. The mass was to be held in the 14th century red schist Gothic church named Notre-Dame-du-Bout-du-Pont and I felt that I needed every prayer I could get, even if it was in Basque. The church is nestled in the small fifteenth century town sitting on the Nive River and above the town is the Citadelle with its cobbled streets running down hill and over the river. I could see all of this from my hotel window and was anxious to begin. I ate a touch of breakfast and was out the door like I owed them money.

As I was sitting in the mass, I felt this overwhelming sense of fear come over me, which stayed with me as I crossed over the bridge leaving the city and entering through the gate to the Camino. I stood looking at the base of the French Pyrenees Mountains and the fear hit me like a wave flowing through and over my body. I was getting ready to take my first step on the Camino and I found myself paralyzed with fear! There are so many people watching me; what if I fail or don't finish!? Who am I to think I can pull something like this off? I'm obese, middle-aged, have a brain tumor and have never hiked any further than the fridge. My body is already hurting from carrying the backpack from Paris to St. Jean, my knees, shoulders bruised, feet; oh God, please be with me! I was reminded of Peter from The Bible. His act of faith in throwing his foot over the boat of fear, in order to walk on water! So, with that thought, I threw my right foot forward and felt a rush which spurned my left foot to follow. As I began to put one foot in front of the other, my tears came forth and I continued to cry for miles. I don't know why!

Today's walk is only 8 km but it's straight up the mountain and my backpack didn't lose any weight overnight at all. My first stop is in a small place called Orrisson. It's a beautiful albergue', which is nestled into the side of a mountain in the Pyrenees. An albergue' or hostel are hotels of a sort but large rooms with many bunk beds in them, barrack style. There is no privacy and most are co-ed. Each one is unique and holds surprises of its own. This albergue' was beautiful! They had built a huge wooden deck which jutted out over the edge of the mountain. The vistas were breathtaking, the singing birds were plenty and the people were nice. I was going to bed right after dinner as I was exhausted! I can't believe I made it to this point but my next lesson was learned here. I thought I had packed only necessities but quickly decided to purge! It's funny what we think is necessary, until we are faced with having to carry it all on our backs, uphill.

I arrived late but entered the bunk room, hoping to find a bottom bunk but they were all taken. While I was making my top bunk my own for the night, I was shocked to see a middle-aged man walk from the shower in the bunk room stark nekked. Oh mercy, I'm in Europe. Next lesson learned, act like you don't see anything. I stayed focused on my tasks at hand and his bare butt wasn't one of them. I gathered my shower items and hit the shower. A token purchased gave me a 5 minute hot shower. Oh, another shower nightmare, don't they know fat girls take longer to shower? It takes me 5 minutes just to get the shampoo out of my hair. Next lesson learned; shower quickly or the water goes ice cold.

I got ready for dinner and upon entering the main dining hall, I saw a beautiful long table filled with table settings, lit candles and fresh flowers. I was shocked by the splendor of the scene; it looked like a set out of an epic movie. Pilgrims began to enter and find their seats. I remained quiet and observant. People of all countries and all walks of life were on this "walk" of a lifetime. Everyone was anxious to hear about others' "why's" for walking but I didn't share, I just listened and soaked everything up. I wasn't rude; just shy and quiet. The food was splendid and I was starving. I ordered food and drink for the next day's journey, said my goodnights and headed to bed.

The night was hot, no fresh air, and lots of snoring kept me awake. I was stripped down to my bra and panties because of the hot night air and I found myself having to go to the bathroom. Being pitch dark, there wasn't light from any source to be able to find my drawers, so I thought to myself... shhhhh... be quiet and nobody will even hear you; they're all asleep. I tiptoed to the bathroom, did my deed and slowly crept back to bed while sporting my favorite skivvies. As I turned the corner, I ran face to face into a man who got up to smoke a cigarette. UGH; now I'm the nudie. Oh well, I'm in Europe. I struggled getting to sleep because of the heat but also because I was full of fear about the following day. Today had been 8 km (4.9 miles) straight up but tomorrow will be 19 km (11.8 miles) and that will be straight up and then straight down! There wouldn't be any places to stay midway, no restaurants, café's, villages or even bathrooms. What am I doing? Fear took over but I remember Peter, no doubts; just do! One step at a time!

CHAPTER 45

I awoke with the sun and a newfound passion. I was excited to accomplish this huge feat and now I was on a mission. I started out the day with my pedometer falling off of my money belt and being flushed into the sewers of France. No, I didn't want to track the miles badly enough to go for it! Breakfast was filling, pilgrims were nice and the path was calling me.

I took my first step with complete commitment but still felt the fear. I decided to feel the fear and push into it by putting one foot in front of the other. Ten km straight up and the last 9 km being straight down and I do mean steep in both directions. The weather was beautiful with bright blue skies, huge puffy white clouds and the sounds of sheep bells echoing throughout the countryside. Within two hours of walking and frequent breaks, I ran across a cow that was within five feet of the fence and giving birth. I stood in disbelief as I watched this miracle unfold. Tears ran down my cheeks as I wondered how I could be so lucky to be the only pilgrim here at this moment in time. Was God allowing me to witness this beauty as a gentle reminder that I'm going through my own rebirth with this walk? Or was I just plain lucky. I took it as sign, thanked God and watched the mother lovingly clean her young. This was beginning of a new me.

I continued my journey, running into pilgrims that were exhausted, out of water, feet full of blisters or just sitting on the sideline watching others pass. I slowly crept my way up the mountaintops making sure to take frequent breaks, drink water, share with those that were dry and tend to pilgrims in trouble with blisters. I'm not a nurse and I didn't have an abundance of water or food, but I wanted to WALK GOD, so others would come to know God.

The day progressed slowly as I gained miles. I found myself excited by reaching a peak, only to find there was another one just ahead. Many miles covered without seeing any pilgrims whatsoever but then I reached what I thought was the top. Upon my arrival, emergency services were there and many pilgrims were around. It seems a pilgrim had a heart attack and died. I didn't see it but saw the aftermath and confusion. People were scared; this became real. It was already real to me as I felt like I was going to die many times throughout the day but had no idea that the latter half of the day would be the worst.

As I started down the 9 km to Roncevalles, Spain, crossing over from France, I found myself on large loose gravel and at a very steep grade. It was hot, the Spanish flies were eating me alive, my legs were weak and I was unsure of my footing. This was beyond miserable. My eyes were nearly swollen shut from crying and sweat dripping into them throughout the day. There wasn't any place to really step aside and take a break and sitting down amidst the path wasn't possible. There weren't any bathrooms to be found and to make matters worse, I had to go. Pilgrims passed me like I was standing still and how do I squat on this steep grade and not be seen by any passersby? Dilemmas continued but my next lesson was learned. Drop, squat and listen quietly for leaves crunching underfoot. Yeah, mastered the art of keeping my backpack on and taking care of business, without anyone seeing a thing!

The last 3 km were the worst. My knees kept buckling, I had welts popping up all over my body from Spanish flies biting and I was utterly exhausted. Passing pilgrims put on the pressure as I was reminded that dinner is at 7 p.m. and I was going to be late if I didn't hurry. Tears began to flow and I was angry. The guidebooks were clear that this part was the worst of all 800 km but it also said that going up was the hardest part. Not true, going down sucked because by then, you're exhausted and sore and your footing is next to impossible. Lies! I was tired, hungry, out of water, bitterly sore and itching all over. I decided to focus on what I wanted to grow, so I began to loudly sing praise songs as I used my walking poles to wildly swat the flies away, to no avail. Before I knew it, a young girl had zipped up next to me and began to talk. It was obvious to her that I was struggling so she said she would finish out the day with me even though she was an expert hiker and could go faster; I think

I might have been an excuse so she could slow down herself. At least that's what I've told myself since. She was a 33 year old newlywed walking alone and from Chicago; the irony. Her new husband was unable to join her due to passport and visa issues. We talked and walked; it was clear that her stride was faster than mine but she lovingly stayed with me. As we entered the city of Roncevalles, Spain, we could see the monastery where we were to stay. It was dedicated to caring for pilgrims and I needed some caring! I just kept focused on putting one foot in front of the other and made it to the bar. I entered the bar and collapsed into a chair and began sobbing in front of everyone. No, I didn't care who saw me; all appearances were a mute point by this time. My new friend celebrated my victory by purchasing a dinner ticket for me and she quickly left to go register and shower. I got myself together, found my bunk but didn't have time for a shower, much to the dismay of my dinner mates I'm sure. As I rounded the courtyard to the dinner hall, lots of people started clapping and got to their feet. Many began to run up to me and congratulate me on my victory. Yes, I was the 300 pound middle-aged woman who hiked over the Pyrenees Mountains that day and lived to tell about it. I took a bow and we all laughed as I nearly fell over. We ate dinner together but I never saw any of those people again, other than my new friend from Chicago. With lights out at 10:00 p.m., I quickly skyped with Tom and the children, posted my victory to Facebook and took a 5 minute hot shower. The pain in my legs kept me from sleeping that night so I wrote a long entry in my journal but had to do it by tiny pin light that I had for emergencies.

Today I mastered the art of peeing on a bush four times without anyone seeing, walked 19 km on severely steep grades (even though it took me 11 hours), met new friends, pushed myself further than I ever physically thought possible, stretched my thinking beyond belief and came out of the birth canal a new person. This was the beginning of a walk to remember but it all started with the first step!

CHAPTER 46

My new friend Jen and I arose late and were the last to leave the monastery. I had no sleep due to severe pain rushing through my body and we were too late for breakfast so walking began. I couldn't believe I was able to walk at all, but we made it to a small medieval village called Espinol which was only 6.5 km (4.03 miles). We stayed in a private hotel for 10 euros each and that gave us private bedrooms plus breakfast the next morning. Jen walked to a market and bought some fresh goat cheese and crackers for breakfast. I slept til 3:00 p.m., ate some more crackers and went back to sleep until 11:15 this next morning. I awakened feeling like a new woman.

Jen and I parted ways as she wanted to walk 32 km today and I wasn't! She was also a real talker and I wanted peace. I also wanted to taxi a bit until I found out it was going to be 45 euros which was around $60 USD. I walked 15.4 km (9.6 miles) to Zubiri, Spain, spent the night and slept hard. I made the decision to avoid walking with other pilgrims. I was called to walk this alone and I had to honor that calling.

Day 5 was a short walk from Zubiri to Akerreta which was only 6.3 km (3.93 miles). I had one tiny blister but my body continued to ache beyond words. It was over 102 degrees today due to a hot pocket that hit from Africa and without knowing this in advance, I had doubled my weight on the modified backpack. Oh my goodness, I am so glad I intended to only go this short distance. I arrived in Akerreta at 10:40 am without issue, stumbled to the door of the home (hotel) and was welcomed by a lovely homeowner of an original house built in 1701. She was on the list as a hotel but only opens her home to walking pilgrims starting in St. Jean and going the distance to Santiago. She didn't allow biking or horseback pilgrims to stay; they were denied entrance. I signed an oath of commitment to finish in Santiago before she would rent out a suite. I did so, paid my 40 euros and got settled into my private suite. With dinner that night, breakfast tomorrow, all beverages and lunch for the trek to Pamplona included. She was absolutely lovely. She took my gear, kissed both cheeks, prayed over me and thanked God for my safe passage, then handed me a nice cold glass of water. Was this love I was seeing from this stranger? Was I possibly seeing God?

Last night while I was in Zubiri, I met a woman from California who said she came on the Camino to find God. I shared some verses about Romans Road with her, on my Ipad and after praying with her (what she was willing to pray), I helped her download an audio Bible onto her Ipad. I told her she'd find God on Romans Road while walking the Camino road, if she was honestly searching and willing to be spoken to by God. I have tears in my eyes as I write this, because today the hotel owner was the first person dedicated to helping pilgrims, that I saw God in. I had already found God many years ago but had genuinely not seen God in other people for a long time; before today. I see God in Tom; his love, gentleness, steadfastness and the fruits of his spirit but <u>really not anyone else for most of my life</u>. I was shocked by this experience and continued to cry as I became fully aware at how my faith in people was at an all time low. So many people who claim to love God, and have God in them, are filled with anger, bitterness, mistrust, self-centeredness, prideful and more concerned with themselves than allowing God to just be seen through them. I ended the day with praying, "Thank you God for this insight and help me to be warm, loving, welcoming and a giving child of Yours. I only desire to please You and by opening myself completely to be used as your vessel; bring others to know You and to love You as I love You. I thank you, Jesus for the removal of all emotional and mental stress / frustrations and I praise you for all things. Please be with Tom and all three children. Keep them safe and make your presence known". Phil. 4:13 KJV – I can do ALL things through Christ which strengthens me. I had an amazing dinner, met a pilgrim couple from Spain that were walking in celebration of his 75th birthday and enjoyed multiple baths in my deep, claw footed, private bathtub. I washed out my clothing, hung it over the balcony to dry for the night, slept peacefully and as I drifted off, my thoughts returned to the owner that morning. I had seen God in the owner of the hotel. This gave me hope but just as there is good; bad is always lurking about ready to pounce; the yin and yang, good and bad, positive and negative; the wife and her husband.

I arose to a beautiful sunrise through my window. I ate breakfast in the hotel alone and began preparing to depart. I started to pack my gear and began looking for my clean clothes which were hanging on the balcony the night before. This morning, they were gone. I hung my head over the edge, only to see that all of my clean clothes were scattered all over the courtyard below. A pilgrim was walking by, saw me looking down and he began to laugh. He didn't speak a lick of English, so my efforts to stop him were futile. He began to pick my clothes up off of the ground and I thought I was going to scream when he got to my underroos; another embarrassing moment on the road to Santiago. I gathered my packed gear, thanked the stranger for coming to my clothing rescue and snapped my backpack in place.

As I was tying my boots for the days hike, an older pilgrim man greeted me, dumped his backpack beside mine and entered the hotel to use the restroom and I assumed to also check into the hotel as a guest. The husband of the owner came outside a few moments later, asked me if it was my gear and I said no. He inquired further but I told him it was owned by the man who was checking in. He gruffly said that no man was checking in and that he was sick and tired of pilgrims wanting to use the restroom. He then grabbed the pilgrims gear, said that he was going to teach him a lesson and took it inside. He instructed me to say nothing about this to the man, if he returned. I was shocked by this but just minded my own business and prepared for the day. Shortly, the man returned to find his sack missing and asked me if I knew what happened to it. I was scared to tell him because the owner's husband was so angry, but after he rang the doorbell three times with no answer, I told him what happened. This was cruel. This older pilgrim was on a quest and to take his pack was just plain cruel. The confused old pilgrim left with his pack, the owner's husband smirked and I felt horribly sad. I told the owner's husband that since the pilgrim will probably never pass again, what lesson was learned. I bravely told him that it was a cruel act, shared how loving and kind his wife was the day before and that walking his own camino might help to soften his own hardened heart. He lowered his head, entered the house and closed the door behind him. I lowered my head and said a short prayer for both the owner's husband and the old pilgrim. My day began with a sad heart and back to square one with my loss of faith in humanity.

CHAPTER 47

Today I was walking 11 km (6.9 miles) to Trinidad de Arre Convent; just before Pamplona. Long strenuous, dangerous paths at times, that were only twelve inches wide and nearly overgrown with bushes, filled my day. I was followed all day by millions of butterflies of all kinds, which made me smile most of the day. I felt like my mother was walking with me.

At one point, I came to a place in the road that offered five types of paths I could choose from. I could proceed on any one of these options and still end up in Pamplona but which way to go? The medieval route sounded interesting to me, so that was my choice. Little did I know, it was a rarely traveled path, and was high in difficulty.

The beautiful, narrow pathway stretched alongside a bubbling brook for a short time, over bridges with creeks and it was amazingly peaceful. I couldn't figure out why the path was so rarely used by hikers and it wasn't even in my guidebook; it was so beautiful and tranquil. All of a sudden it became clear. I began to notice that the path narrowed and was only eight inches wide, quite overgrown and without forewarning everything changed with no chance of retreating. The right side of the path was suddenly framed by a cliff that went straight up and eight inches to the left of the cliff was a steep cliff that jutted straight down to the river below. Jagged rocks lined the eight inch wide path way, there was no place to sit down and not enough room for me to even use my walking sticks for balance. Quickly this became very dangerous. I was the only pilgrim for miles and as I trudged the long dangerous stretch, the eight inch path began to get very steep. I started passing crosses and shrines that were imbedded in the cliff side to my right, as a testament to pilgrims who lost their lives walking this path and some were recent deaths. This was more than unnerving and the path seemed to be never-ending. Too dangerous to stop, not enough room to sit down, unable to balance or use my poles, backpack weighing very heavily, bending over just to make it up the steep path and running out of water. It was only supposed to be a 6.9 km walk to the convent but this was much further than that. I began to feel light-headed, and out of breath, so I started to pray out loud. I thought, I'm in trouble here. No water, no food left, not feeling well and nowhere close to Trinidad! My legs were giving out but there was no place to sit and rest so I just kept a hand on the cliff, leaning against it from time to time, just to catch my breath. I couldn't go on much further... I continued to pray aloud with each step I took until I didn't even have the breath for that; my prayers became silent. It had been nearly two miles of a steep, dangerous climb with no water and I was going down; I could feel it. I sucked hard on my water tube but it was bone dry and had been for quite some time. I was desperate now but I kept a positive mindset. I knew that I was in my last few steps of energy, when all of a sudden my last step possible put me at the top; into the most beautiful lush green grassy clearing. I fell to my knees and I remember thinking, this must be heaven!

I must have lost consciousness because the next thing I knew was that ice cold water was being poured onto my face. I cupped my hand and greedily drank my fill, as I cried like a child. I kept thinking that at any moment the water could disappear. As I cleared the water and tears out of my eyes, I looked up and there was a woman dressed in an all white dress and head covering. She was pouring water onto my face from what looked like an ancient pitcher. I thought I had died, gone to heaven and Mother Mary was giving me water, from the eternal spring. I could've sworn it was Mary. I said thank you to her and she dropped the pitcher and ran. I called out for her to stop… please but she kept going. I hadn't seen any other pilgrims on the whole path today and there weren't any other pilgrims around but as I collapsed back into the lush green cool grass; thanking God for the water and rest, even if it was in heaven. Shortly the woman in white re-emerged, followed by a woman in a light blue long dress and head covering. The woman in blue asked me if I was okay, in English. I asked her if this was heaven and she laughingly said, "No, but we like to think it is." She asked me if I needed food but I couldn't even speak, I could only cry. How is it that God knows when we can't take a step further on our own or that our spring has run dry? How is it that I am worthy enough for Him to meet my needs at that very moment? Thank you Jesus for loving a sinner, such as I.

She continued to give me water, sat on the grass with me and we began to talk. I looked around and saw a partial church standing that looked really old. It was beautifully maintained and I just listened to her captivating voice.

CHAPTER 48

She was a nun and her name was Sarah. Sister Sarah. The building was a seventh century church and a convent of nuns resided there with their only mission; to care for the full needs of the pilgrims that chose to walk the medieval road (the hardest way).

The church was bare and simple, yet amazingly beautiful. She took me by the hand, helped me to my feet and we walked inside the church. They had bright green arrow-shaped post-it notes that pilgrims could write a prayer on and stick it to an area surrounding a crucifix. I added mine to the others that had taken this route in May – June and although it was full, it wasn't many for a whole two month period of time. My prayer was, "Please help me to be a child that glorifies You Lord – in all ways. I love You Father God and pray that each person that crosses my path sees you in me!"

Sister Sarah and I sat down inside the church and started a conversation that would last for over ninety minutes. I shared that I know that I am forgiven and that God walks with me. She smiled and said that she could see that I knew "the truth". She took out her Spanish Bible and took me to and through Romans Road. With a smile on her face, she shared that she is forgiven too! All the while, a twenty-something year old Korean boy had joined us and was quietly listening to the conversation. I'm not sure when he walked into the church or where he even came from; he didn't have a backpack and was not dressed to walk the path. The church was in the middle of nowhere, with only the path to give one access. He had tears running down his cheeks as we were praying together, so I reached out my hand and grasped his. He began to openly weep and he didn't even speak English. God's love and truth has a language all its own and I knew he understood every word being spoken. The young boy rose and disappeared; neither of us figuring out where he had gone.

Sister Sarah asked me why I am walking the Camino de Santiago and again, I started to weep. I told her that initially I was walking so as to detach and allow myself some time to unwind but that my main reason has changed. I told her that I came on the Camino to re-charge my God battery. I try to live for God but have lost my faith in God's people. I explained that so many have bled me dry, treated me badly and talk a big walk but don't walk it. She began to weep and said that she too was concerned for the Church for the same reasons. We talked on and on and by the end, she said that each night the convent held a prayer vigil and she said that she would pray out my name. She also said that the nuns could pray aloud for a pilgrim who touched their heart during the day and had opened their eyes. She said that I was that pilgrim today. I thanked her and we just sat and held hands as we wept together. Sarah offered to feed and shelter me for the night, but I felt compelled to press on. We hugged, kissed cheeks, cried and prayed again before departing. This experience was beyond touching. God had revealed Himself to me today. I walked away refreshed, recharged, rehydrated, restocked and praising God. Catholic nuns sharing Romans Road and the Gospel of Christ, in the middle of nowhere; how amazing that is. Although I instinctually knew it was wrong, I grew up being taught that any other "religion", other than ours, was wrong and those people were hell bound! Come judgment day, there are going to be a lot of surprised people; from every religion!

CHAPTER 49

As I continued my journey along the medieval path to Trinidad de Arre, Spain, I passed abandoned ancient stone buildings that were being consumed by the land whence they came from and gorgeous flowering bushes. From the moment my boot set foot on the path, I was being surrounded by millions of butterflies of all colors and species. This was overwhelmingly beautiful and I felt this all-consuming feeling of my mother's presence, as well as God's. The peace was incredible and the walk was easy.

Three to four km into the walk, I came across a Spanish man on a donkey, selling fruit and water out of a cooler. All I could do was laugh. God had a sense of humor and I believe in supporting the small business man, so I bought a banana, orange, grapes and water from him. Where did this man come from? There weren't any roads and a donkey? I sat down and the man sat with me while I ate my goodies. His name was Jose' and he told me all about the special bushes that lined the medieval path and how these bushes attract butterflies from all over the world. He said they migrate to this area and that I was here at the perfect time. He asked me why I was walking this treacherous journey so once again, I shared. He said that he loved God too and just smiled.

Within minutes, two young men walked out of nowhere and were so grateful to see someone with water. They ordered two bottles of water from the man and handed him a twenty euro bill. The man said no; he didn't have change for that but the young men had already opened and drank from the bottles. The man became angry when he realized the young men didn't have any smaller amounts of euros and started to scream at the boys. I just reached into my money belt, took out five euros and bought the water for the boys along with an extra bottle each and some fruit for their journey. The young men were shocked as was the man but I just said, "A while ago, God met my needs so why wouldn't I meet yours? Consider this a gift on the Camino de Santiago". I smiled, thanked the man, wished the boys a "Buen Camino", which is well-wishing for their journey, and I moved on.

Within an hour of walking, the boys caught up to me and yelling for me to please wait. I did so and they couldn't thank me enough. One of them told me that I was his angel, sharing that they had been out of water for many hours and were both scared. They told me they were 21 and 22 years old, from Iceland and came on the Camino because they had lost faith in humanity. I thought how is it possible, for a 21 year old boy, to lose faith in humanity at such a young age. What could he have experienced that was so bad for him to lose faith in all of humanity? They told me that my kindness was the first act of goodness they had witnessed for a long time. I felt saddened at the thought. They shared that they were slow to catch up with me because the man on the donkey kept them talking about my kind act and how he himself doesn't see nice things very often. Again, I felt sad. I came on the Camino to restore my faith in God's people but how glorious that God is using me to do that for others. God met my needs and within an hour, I not only had enough for myself but I was able to meet the needs of someone else. I understood, hugged them both and grabbed their hands as we began to all three walk together. We walked arm in arm for the next 4-5 km. They were kind young boys who were jovial, had great laughs and talked about loving others, kindness and how humanity has to begin within us. When we came to the medieval bridge in Trinid, the boys informed me they were going on to Pamplona and asked me to join them. I thanked them for the offer but that I was done. Today had been very taxing physically and I had a bed waiting for me in the convent. We hugged, took pictures and joyfully waved as we said our good-byes. I never saw the boys again but am grateful for the tender interaction.

    I made it to Trinidad de Arre and the convent was amazing. It stood right next to the old stone bridge and looked like something out of an Excalibur movie. I knocked on a huge old door and a short, bald, Spanish-speaking priest welcomed me to the ancient church with a wave of his hand and without speaking a word, he smiled, took my 6 euro for the bed and ushered me to my bunk. No wifi, dinner, breakfast, hot water or vending machines; primitive is an understatement but I loved it! Large uneven stone floors with planked wood pews, a gorgeous altar and the most beautiful courtyard filled with a myriad of flowers and sweet little tables with wooden chairs. I washed out my walking clothes for the day, hung them to dry, aired out my boots and without showering, was in bed asleep by 5 p.m.

I woke at 7:50 a.m. to two English speaking women in the room; the newly converted Catholic from Connecticut and the angry, aggressive teacher from New York. The second she saw my eyes open, she yelled at me, telling me how badly I snored and how she had to move outside just to sleep. I apologized but quickly dismissed her aggressive attitude; refusing to take it on as my own. With no breakfast in sight, I began packing my gear and quickly realized that somewhere along the walk I had lost my hygiene bag. I laughed out loud, asked my roomies if they had seen a bright pink bag laying somewhere on the path and they both said yes. When I asked if they picked it up, the Catholic convert said, "Oh I feel so guilty because I thought about it but just left it.

The angry teacher said, "Hell no, it wasn't my crap." I just laughed again at the irony of their comments and prepped to leave. I bid them a "Buen Camino" and was on my way to Pamplona.

CHAPTER 50

A casual 5.2 km (3.2 miles) to Pamplona ended on sleepy streets desolate of life. Hungry and ready to check into my albergue' but found that it wasn't opening until noon. The city was preparing for the "Running of the Bulls" week and within an hour, city workers were installing barricades for the bulls and emergency service tents were erected with workers collecting funds to help provide medical attention to those who get hurt while running FROM the bulls. My first thought was a country with an astronomical rate of unemployment and poor economy and yet there were funds for this? Very interesting to walk the streets of Pamplona and watch the city wake up and come to life. I checked into my hostel at noon sharp, locked up my gear, claimed my bottom bunk, took a shower and was off to explore the city further.

I found myself in the Toros Arena watching them prepare for bull fighting and eating hot churros with rich chocolate sauce. Streets were narrow and businesses were aplenty. Street performers were out in droves and the drinking began. I could not believe how much these people partied; it was a strange culture to me. A suffering economy but nothing opened before 10 a.m. and all throughout Spain, everything closed up and the streets became desolate from 2-4 p.m. for siesta. From 4 p.m. into the dark night, people celebrated with gross amounts of alcohol and out of control behavior. No wonder the economy was suffering, nobody was working and everyone was drunk. After eating my way through the streets of Pamplona, I tried to get some sleep but even on Ambien, sleep wasn't going to happen because of the crazy partying in the streets outside the window. I waited until the streets were quiet and around 3:50 a.m, I left the hostel and began my day's journey. I loved walking at night because the stars blanketed the sky, the night air was cool and the Spanish flies weren't biting, plus I didn't have to deal with other pilgrims. I found the night air to be cold this night; very cold but I was over Pamplona.

The streets were once again filthy and smelled of liquor so strongly that it made me nauseous. Empty bottles strewn everywhere, condoms on the ground and people lying about on park benches; drunk I'm sure. I couldn't wait to get out of Pamplona and I have no desire to return. My goal for the day was 15 miles so off I went.

As my day progressed, I started noticing that people weren't being very friendly. I was stared at, avoided and even downright ignored in cafés, but I just figured that my experience in Pamplona might be affecting my attitude. Knowing that you attract what you put out, I changed my attitude and started listening to my audio Bible again. Once again I had a smile on my face, peace in my heart and my boot on the path. One foot in front of the other!

I went further than I thought I would and ended up in Puente La Reina Spain; which was 21.6 km (13.5 miles). It was totally opposite of Pamplona. It was quaint, beautiful and clean. All of the straight laced village women stared at my tight hiking pants, bright green shirt and fiery red hair and shunned me as if I was a prostitute or alien. I checked into my hotel and went to the street front tables for tapas (appetizers). A small group of stiff-necked, monotone and neutrally dressed women grabbed the chair out of my hand and they all sat at the table. I was shocked but everywhere I went I was treated like this so I went to a Mercado (market) to buy food and returned to my room. The staring was extreme and ridiculous. After eating lunch, I went to a church for mass. I walked in and everyone in the church turned and stared at me. I walked to an aisle and sat down at the end of the pew. A row of 8-9 older Spanish women dressed in long black skirts, with head coverings on, leaned over, looked down at me and as if it were planned and on cue, they all stood to their feet and moved all of the way down to the other end of the pew. I couldn't help but wonder what was going on! I took a shower so I don't' smell, I am dressed in tight hiking clothing but that shouldn't justify this treatment. Am I imagining this? Oh my goodness, it feels like high school might if you were surrounded by "mean girls." This was crazy.

After mass, the priest approached me and asked to speak with me. I agreed and thanked him for the beautiful service. He spoke English clearly and the exchange was nice. He told me that he noticed what happened with the older women and suggested that I wear a hat. When I asked why, he proceeded to inform me that in this part of Spain, only prostitutes have bright red hair. I asked him to repeat what he had just said, so he did. REALLY? I was born with this hair and now it is a brightly lit neon sign saying I'm open for business? Oh Lord! Well, that explained everything. I thanked him for the information and hurriedly returned to the hotel.

No wifi to be found anywhere in the city and I wish I could talk to Tom. This shunning reminds me of my college years with my family and it's not easy. I also can't seem to shake all of the recent betrayals in my life. Lesson… things aren't always as they seem. 432.9 miles to Santiago!

CHAPTER 51

Today I walked to a medieval mountaintop village that was amazing; beautifully preserved with narrow winding streets and houses with ornate family crests, flower boxes brimming with cascading colors and incredible balconies. The village square was centered around two churches that dated back to the thirteenth century. It was called Cirauqui and all of the homes were closely scattered over the mountain with the most beautiful vistas, that peeked over the tall medieval stone walls that enveloped its village center.

I had a hitch hiker today and low and behold, it was the Catholic convert who roomed with me in Trinidad de Arre. It turns out that she is a "confused" middle-aged, catholic convert with many issues. I chose to stop here for the night because to be completely open, I had to ditch this drama-filled, confused chick. She was so incredibly negative and complained the whole 8.2 km. I cared about her and wanted to give but found myself having my own aches and pains; her complaints seemed to make my hurts, hurt more. I was done!

I ate like a pig, showered liked I'd never had hot water, slept like a baby and talked to nobody. I awoke with a refreshed body, renewed spirit and ate breakfast like I wouldn't have food for days. As I walked out of town, I noticed the most amazing display on the mountainside. The villagers had taken all of their old tires and created a huge map of the world, honoring pilgrims from all over. This was beautiful and pictures were a must. Within 5 minutes from the village walls, I began to walk on medieval Roman road. It was amazingly preserved and I had chills run through my body as I thought of the millions of pilgrims who had walked on these very stones for thousands of years.

By noon I passed a group of pilgrims eating lunch on the side of the path. Who was it? It was the angry teacher from New York and the middle-aged confused Catholic convert! **OMG**... I felt like I had toilet paper stuck to the bottom of my shoe and I just couldn't shake it off. I smiled, gave a wave and the angry teacher asked me if I was too good to stop and eat with them. I laughed and said, "Girl, you're so silly, enjoy your lunch" and I kept on walking. The last thing I wanted to do was taint my quest with negative, angry, confused, complaining people but wanted to make sure that my spirit was kind.

The next few days were filled with ice cold rain. I trudged through mud, shin deep water and I was freezing to the bone.

The wind whipped over the plains but I had to push on. I knew this was only temporary but it just didn't stop. I huddled next to buildings, sheltered myself underneath bridges and hadn't seen any pilgrims other than my own reflection. Where was everyone? I figured they were hiding out in albergues' and hostels until the rain passed but I had to press on. I made the commitment from the beginning to never stay in one village or city for longer than one night and the little villages I've stayed in didn't have any other pilgrims there. I hadn't had wifi for days due to the storms and I didn't want to worry Tom, so I pressed on. The last night, I was forced to sleep underneath a bridge, because of the storm and felt that my life had come full circle. I awoke early and continued.

I finally made it to a tiny village and the café there had wifi. It had been 5 days of ice cold rain, treacherous terrain, unreal conditions and no Tom! I couldn't wait to skype him. I cried and cried! I was cold and wet to the bone, felt sick and kept being treated as if I was a prostitute. The shunning was ridiculous but certainly causing me to deal with unresolved issues with my family. I felt like I was being cut down; stripped to the bone! I was glad that he hadn't called the American Embassy in Spain because he hadn't heard from me. Tom told me to just take a train or bus to get out of the bad weather and the part of Spain that was not redhead friendly; some people were too friendly. He told me that nobody we would ever know would do as much as I've done, so not to feel badly, just get out! I agreed and just as quickly realized that I was going to have to WALK a good 10 miles in order to even find a bus station. Ugh! 10 miles later, I found a hotel, café and a bus station. I ate a hot dinner, took a hot shower and downloaded pictures to Facebook. Within minutes I started getting pings from people who were following me and giving me words of support. I was shocked by this because my Facebook posts were for my children and Tom; not thinking that other people would see them too. People started making comments that thanked me for being so courageous and brave. They said that I was inspiring them to get off of the sofa and make changes in their lives. People said that I was doing it for them because they could never take an adventure like this due to bad knees or other physical limitations. Something shifted inside me. I started this journey, doing it for me, now I was going to push through, for them! And in the process, I would be helping me. After a good long cry and a good long, hard sleep, I awoke with a new passion! I laced up my boots, grabbed my backpack and walked out into the rain. Funny what we can do when we have a good "why" and really set our minds to it. Anything is possible.

CHAPTER 52

It had been nearly a week of hard, cold rain and today wasn't any different. I was walking over 25 miles today in order to get to the next village and the weather was brutal. It felt like I had trudged the full distance but it had only been six miles due to the torrential downpour, mud and steep paths. I had fallen several times and my gear was soaked through and through, caked with mud. The weather got worse really fast with a cold hard wind that accompanied the cold rain and I found myself again, unable to go any further, but there was nowhere to take cover. I had no choice but to continue and with a turn of a bend, I saw a barn.

I approached the barn with a desperate need for cover and warmth but found it blocked with some sort of strange lock. I shimmied it off the door and quickly secured it behind me; grateful for the shelter from the storm. There wasn't a farmhouse within sight but I felt I had no choice; for my own safety. I made a thick bed out of fresh hay, stripped off my wet clothes and boots, hung them to dry and took out a dry set of clothing that I had kept in a waterproof bag. I wrapped myself in my emergency blanket, covered myself in fresh hay and in no time flat, I started to get warm. With plenty of water and some dry snacks, my afternoon passed quickly and I fell asleep with contentment.

The warmth of the morning sunlight woke me, as it hit my face, while coming through a tiny window pane. As I opened my eyes, I heard a cocking of a shotgun! I felt a wave of fear rush through my body as I focused my vision, only to see a farmer have a shotgun pointed at me. He began to yell at me in Basque (not Spanish) and I jumped up with my hands in the air. He continued to yell at me as I grabbed my gear and as soon as he saw the shell hanging from my backpack (symbolizing that I am a pilgrim), he put the gun down and patted me on the back. I started to cry and he just kept patting my back and went to the door and yelled for someone. Through the door walked an older woman in a long black dress carrying a basket of vegetables. Her face was full of wrinkles and character. She smiled, as he pointed to my shell and they both took my arm and my gear as they directed me outside. I went from feeling like I was going to be shot and buried right here, to meeting new friends. They walked me through a clump of trees and a tiny little stone house appeared. She walked ahead very quickly and opened the front door, laid her basket on the table and waved me indoors.

The tiny little house looked like a set from "Little House on the Prairie". There was a blazing fire in the fireplace with a kettle hanging near it. An old wooden table with four chairs was in the center of the room and a hand pump for water fed into the old sink underneath the window. There was an earthy smell about the place. They were both very friendly with lots of pats on the back and he rambled on in Basque; which I clearly didn't understand. She gave me a cup of some kind of hot tea, which was delicious, and I sipped it as I sat closely to the fire. She hurriedly made eggs, ham and homemade rolls with fresh butter for the three of us. I hadn't noticed but this sweet woman had taken all of my gear out in the other room and there was a fire going in that room that had been drying my things out. I was thrilled! I smiled and kept saying thank you in English but they fully understood without understanding the language. Funny what can be accomplished with pats on the back, smiles, nods and handshakes; a universal language that bridges gaps in any country! Pictures were taken, hugs were exchanged and I left well rested, dry, a full tummy, fully restocked and bright blue skies overhead. Today was going to be a great day and I saw God today in two elderly villagers, on the Camino de Santiago.

CHAPTER 53

A full day of casual walking and the heat was a nice change; although that meant that the Spanish biting flies were out in droves and they wanted me! I passed sheep farmers that ushered their flocks down the Camino path, tons of huge rolls of hay tucked into the rolling hills of the countryside, big white puffy clouds and other pilgrims. It was a casual walk over those rolling hills and casual conversations with others. From time to time, I would stop alongside the path and take a break to rest my feet, air out the boots and grab some nutrition. This was changing for me; food had gone from something that curbs the emotions or stress to something that was used to provide fuel for my body to be able to continue the walk. That was a huge change that was occurring! I also noticed that I wasn't using any salt and everything was fresh. No canned goods, no sodas, no pre-made boxed goods, just wholesome fresh food and water; with the occasional Spanish coffee of course.

I ended my day in a gorgeous albergue that was in a 510 year old renovated stone winery. It was breathtaking to say the least. It was in Villatuerta, just over the medieval bridge and up on the side of the little hill. The owners were lovely and I will never forget all of the colorful hammocks hanging in the covered wraparound porch. Here I had my first taste of paella, which is a rice dish originally from Valencia, Spain and thoroughly enjoyed the pilgrim dinner that the owner prepared for us. The pilgrims that were there that night were lovely, positive and a joy to be around. After a full meal, lots of laughter, a great hot shower and a great Skype call with Tom and the children, I was ready to take on the next day! One step at a time!

I awoke in the morning really sore so I decided to take a shower. I went to get my hygiene bag and someone had taken it. Wow; I guess they stank more than I did, so after I had a tinge of anger run through my blood, I laughed and took out my emergency travel hygiene bag. I got a great shower, had a great breakfast and headed out!

It was another beautiful day of bright blue skies and it was hot already! Within minutes I began to sweat, which usually meant that the biting flies were going to eat me alive but they weren't bothering me much! What was this about? After a full day of walking in 103 degree heat and only a couple of bites, I figured out that they had been attracted to my body wash. I saw God again today on the Camino de Santiago in the mercy He gave me when He allowed someone to steal that body wash. Sad part is that person was now being eaten alive. Natural consequences of our choices abound and I just laughed at the irony. I said a quick prayer for that person and finished out the day, walking alone by choice with only two new bites! Praise God.

I stopped for the day in what appeared to be a decent hostel but turned out to be pretty rough! The staff was really rude to pilgrims and the price was ridiculous but there was wifi, hot showers, a bare bunk bed and a food source, so no complaints. I downloaded pictures to face book and got a message from an old college friend named Benito.

He told me that his mother has a pension' just two hours from where I was staying that night but she was leaving in two days to go visit him in New York. Her pension' wasn't on the Camino path but she was so close that not going wasn't an option. I was thrilled to hear from him and couldn't resist the offer to visit her, so the next morning I hopped a bus and the ride was a real treat. I arrived and although she didn't speak a lick of English, we communicated via an online translation service. It was a delightful visit and her home was beautiful. We skyped with Benito and tears flowed. What a beautiful gift God gave us all and I was grateful. With a quick bus ride back to my last location the next morning, my walk continued!

I continued to be treated as if I were a prostitute because of my red hair and I just kept thinking how strange cultures are. A simple color of hair, which you are born with, sets one apart as a lady of the night, a simple shell hanging from a backpack makes you special, very interesting facts which made no sense to me and yet they were both true. I felt this treatment begin to erode my attitude and energy. Sadly but I recognized that this treatment would have caused me to quit long before the torrential downpour for eight days straight would have. I kept putting one foot in front of the other with my eye set on the next village.

CHAPTER 54

I came to this tiny little village called Ciruena. There wasn't much there other than a beautiful old church and some dilapidated old buildings but there was a bar that served food. I was hungry so I stopped but it was siesta time and everything was closed. I noticed a little pension' called Casa Victoria and it looked really nice, so I rang the bell and a nice woman answered the door. She had short dark hair and wore glasses, but also had a smile from ear to ear. I said, "Peregrino pension'?" and she just smiled. She ushered me inside and I paid her my 20 euros for the night. That bought me a private bedroom and bathroom; I was thrilled. When I saw the room, I became tearful. It was on the top floor, had steep sloped ceilings, a huge bed with hand-carved swans on the head and footboard and looked like something out of a magazine. The bathroom was huge, clean and all mine! I was in heaven.

After I showered and changed, I rested then went downstairs for food. By this time the bar had reopened and I was there as it was the only place in the village to get something to eat. I ordered something from the server that I seemed to be bothering and when it came, there was a bug in it, so I just pushed it back away from me. I paid for it, bought a bag of chips and left. When I returned to the pension so quickly, they inquired by using a translator and I told them what happened. I spent the evening talking at great length to Maria and Paxti; the owners of the pension. They were truly lovely people and we continue to be friends to this day. Their kindness recharged my batteries and got me through my frustrations. It seems that my reaching this far, pushed me through the area of Spain that had the wrong idea about redheads. Whew, I was done with that!

I suggested that Maria offer pilgrims a dinner so they wouldn't have to deal with the only bar in town and she thought she might not be able to do that in her tiny kitchen but I encouraged her with ideas that would work. From that point forward, the bar wasn't the only place that pilgrims could be fed but Maria's kitchen was the best. She makes paella and many other delicious meals for her guests and the best breakfast that I got on the Camino! Casa Victoria is a stop that every pilgrim should afford themselves. It was my oasis in the desert. Maria and Paxti were my encouragement at the moment it was needed! Thank you to my dear friends. After hugs and pictures, another day on the Camino de Santiago and my big walk continues!

Another day of 102 degree heat in the shade and there wasn't any shade. Approximately 8 km into walking, I met up with two men that were walking together. Michael was 53 years old and from Cambridge, while Jacque was 22 and from Toulouse, France. Michael shared that 3 weeks before he and his wife were to begin their walk, his wife died in her sleep. He began to get choked up as he spoke about her and decided to continue with the plans anyway. He lovingly said that he was walking in honor of her.

Jacque remained quiet, was walking barefooted with full gear and if that wasn't enough of a clue, shortly it became clear that there was more to his story. After 6 km of walking with them, Michael stopped for the night but after Jacque and I said our good-byes to Michael, we continued on. It was still early in the day and I wanted to go at least 35 km (21.75 miles) that day, so off we went. As the kilometers began to pass, Jacque began to open up to me without solicitation. He told me that he's been walking every route of the French Camino for 1 ½ years without any money and picking grapes for food. He was absolutely filthy and occasionally he'd talk to himself. After a long listen and observation, I became acutely aware that Jacque was schizophrenic. He proceeded to tell me that over eighteen months earlier his parents announced that they could no longer deal with his mental issues, so they packed up his things in a backpack and threw him and his gear to the street. He started to cry, sharing that he missed his parents but couldn't help having the voices in his head and medications weren't working. I was right in my train of thinking but also knew that with that illness, complete unpredictability and potential violence could accompany him. I took no chances and was astutely aware of his every move. The kilometers, the heat and this level of hyper-vigilance were utterly exhausting but I felt compelled to stay with him. The big walk and small talk continued.

CHAPTER 55

After walking 32 km (19.88 miles) together, I was getting tired but Jacque seemed like he was raring to go. I was ready to drop but every time we entered a village, I entertained staying but I was unable to stop, compelled to proceed with him. Why? I was out of water and there wasn't a village or water hole in sight, when one did show. Why is it that I was afraid to walk to it and refill just because he wasn't? Why? Water and rest is a necessity of life but I wasn't meeting my needs for him. Why? My body screamed, yes, but a new wind would come over me and a deep seeded compulsion to carry on by Jacque's side took over. How could his parents have done that? What got so bad that they were willing to basically abandon their son in his time of need? Aren't they worried, fearful or even care? My heart was being torn; my body being drained beyond belief and yet I had to stay with him. Everyone had given up on him. I don't owe him anything or even know him but I just can't do the same.

We came to a small village and I offered to buy us dinner and with a humble look in his eyes, he graciously thanked me in French, words gently uttered as if unworthy to even speak. I was so grateful because I was parched and hungry as ever. I served him his food, put my hand on his back, said grace for the food and prayed for his heart and his cure. When I was done, he looked up at me with tear filled eyes; eyes speaking words that his lips were unable to utter. He looked me straight in the eyes and said, "You are love." I asked him what he meant and he just explained that he sees me as love. I got a big lump in my throat and heaviness in my chest; wanting to break down and just sob… but opted to keep it together. A stranger on the Camino sees me as love. Dear God, this is what I want… others to see you through and in me!

He asked if he could travel with me so I agreed but with boundaries in place that I would stop when I must, for any reason, he would accept that without issue, choose to remain and wait, or move on and that we would part by his choosing, not mine. He agreed that if he did something that made me uncomfortable, his choice to do that would be his choice to move on. He held it together and the whole journey was filled with contemplation, confusion, fear, wonder, self-exploration and most of all, thoughts about my daughter, Lindsay. She was diagnosed with schizophrenia as a young child and he was shocked when I shared that with him; I think it gave him hope. My biggest fear, as her mother, was that someday her illness would take her into the homeless community; my heart was breaking for Jacque and worry about "Lindsay's" wellbeing.

The last night before leaving for Paris, Lindsay chose to do something that devastated her father and I. It was an impulsive act that left us feeling betrayed and resulted in Tom's stress, running around and trying to get it resolved. Even though she doesn't have lapses in reality at this point, she still struggles with impulsivity, poor judgment and extremely low self-esteem, all which lead to poor choices and rough consequences. Dear Lord, help me to come to peace with it and give us clear vision for our future role with her! I will not throw her to the streets but I will also not enable this behavior to continue. God has a plan for her life but she is choosing to make bad choices that directly affect us. With these thoughts, my skin began to itch, I felt trembling throughout my body and my heart began to race. I am at a loss and so confused. My body has huge visceral reactions and I cannot continue like this!

As my mind was racing, my heart was hurting and my feet were walking, I began to realize that I wasn't stopping to eat because Jacque wasn't hungry and he didn't want to stop. I wasn't stopping to restock water because he didn't want to and I was scared of losing track of him. I offered to buy his bunk and dinner for the night and he graciously accepted; thank God! I had to stop but wasn't able to let go of this young schizophrenic man. We found a hostel, restocked provisions, showered and ate like crazy people. He rambled throughout dinner, sharing every thought imaginable and I just kindly listened. I made sure his bunk was above mine so that if he got up in the middle of the night to leave, I would feel him and be able to go with him. I didn't sleep all night, after walking 52.9 km (32.9 miles) today. My body was aching, I was exhausted but my fear of losing him kept me from getting the rest I needed. Why did I push myself so hard to walk so far today? My mind kept racing and my anxiety increased.

At 5:10 a.m. Jacque rose and jumped to his feet. He grabbed his gear, didn't say a word to me and headed for breakfast. I grabbed mine, laced up my boots since I was already dressed for the day and followed him. We enjoyed breakfast and I overstocked my provisions for the day. I wasn't sure how far I could walk today without any sleep but I was going for the long haul.

We passed through village after village and the heat was unbearable. I was utterly exhausted but Jacque walked with a vengeance. He shared all about his childhood and how people judged him and his family because of his strange behavior, how people would abuse him because he was different and defective a sense of deep sadness was in his voice at all times. He talked about experiences he'd had on the Camino and the abuse he'd even endured by pilgrims and villagers alike. He told me that he stopped believing in God a long time ago and I walked through my quiet tears.

His feet were a mess! With cuts, dirt and calluses, so as I ran across a pair of abandoned boots, I grabbed them and gave them to him along with a pair of socks that I purchased in a village; he was beyond thrilled. I cannot imagine walking this insanely rough terrain in bare feet. We attended mass together in a small village and afterwards I spoke with the priest about Jacque. Jacque agreed to talk with the priest but when the priest offered help to him, Jacque refused. He said he'd had help from people of God but it always came with a heavy price. I'm not sure what experience he'd had with church help but it was bad enough that he'd rather walk aimlessly and barefooted than return to it.

We had walked over 61 km (37.9 miles) today through the flat, dry meseta and I was ready to drop. Everything was hurting and it was apparent to Jacque that I was really struggling. He turned to me, put his hand on my hand and said, "It's ok, everybody always leaves me anyway." I felt like I was going to vomit and yet these words pierced my heart like none other. I asked him if I could slow down the pace and he agreed, so our walk together continued.

I feel like I'm caught here with Jacque. If I stop, he'll feel that one more person gave up on him and I'll lose him but if I stay, I run the risk of losing myself and not meeting my needs. It's the same with Lindsay. I am caught in a thistle bush where every turn I find myself being hurt and not making any headway to be free of the painful restriction. Do I break free for my own selfish needs or do I just succumb to it and allow it to erode who I am over time. I'm so tired and the pain is so great but God put these people in my life and I had to do that justice! What was justice? This was a question that I was searching to answer. I had to make sure that I was doing right by me, doing right by those I love and being right with God.

Jacque offered to stop and camp for the night together but that would be a risky situation on my part so I graciously passed. We took a water break and I realized we were only 9 km (5.6 miles) from Castrojeriz, Spain. The dirt path was going to be crossing over the paved road just ahead so I gathered myself up and we walked further. As we approached, there was a bus stop and I knew that I couldn't go on any further. We agreed that we would meet at a certain hostel in Castrojeriz and we promised each other to up meet there. By this time, I had walked over 64 km (39.8 miles) without any sleep the night before and I was done!

The bus came and after sitting and waiting for ten minutes, I could barely stand, let alone walk. Jacque helped me on the bus and with significant tears from us both, we bid each other ado. As the bus pulled away, his ongoing wave said it all. I would never see this young man again! I was overcome with guilt, shame and thoughts that I was just one more person who had abandoned him. I sobbed aloud all of the way to the city of Castrojeriz. I checked myself into the hostel and waited outside for his arrival for many hours. He never came!

The next five days were filled with walking and non-stop crying. It didn't matter who was around, where I was or what the scenery was like I couldn't stop crying. Skype calls with Tom were helpful but it became incredibly clear that God allowed Jacque to cross my path! Our walk together was enlightening to me and I hope, helpful to him. I have spent my life dedicated to helping others, even at the sacrifice of my own needs! Letting go of Jacque was as if I was letting go of Lindsay. I can't control her decision, choices and consequences any further. This had to stop. I was done but not done crying.

CHAPTER 56

After five days of crying and walking, I got fresh cherries and other supplies and proceeded to the only hostel with available beds – Sisters of the cleanly heart! These chicks don't know what clean means. This place was scary and dirty. I'll be okay but good Lord, what did I expect for 1 euro. I skyped with Tom and Jonathan, which was great. I was still down about Jacque so I'm sure I was negative; not being the best company. Tom told me that I needed to reserve a special hotel in Santiago and I was stoked. Wooohooo. I spent the evening eating fresh Spanish cherries and went to dinner.

I ran into a family of self-consumed, rude Presbyterian ministers, which happened to live in my home town. I couldn't get over how big they were talking God but how quickly their walk shifted, with time and wine. Their loud antics kept the whole hostel awake until nearly 2 a.m; very Christ-like, as mentioned by a pilgrim from England. I felt sad and angry and fell asleep while eating cherries and praying for them.

Another day of walking... wheat field after wheat field and although I felt bored by the view, I pondered the idea that even the repetition was part of some lesson. The peaceful quiet I was feeling was deafening but welcomed all the same. My thoughts vacillated between Jacque and Lindsay and I put one foot in front of the other to cover miles. I ended the day in another convent that was run by Sisters of the Cleanly Hearts but these sisters were dirtier than last night's chicks. I ate dinner and was going to bed right as "lights out" was called. After ten minutes of sitting in a chair, pondering how in God's name I ended up here, a moderately sized rat crossed the floor and underneath an adjoining bunk. I, being horrified to ever see this at a Marriott, promptly grabbed my things and exited said fine establishment as if it were on fire! Knowing that all other options were no longer an option, I set foot to trail, not really concerned with or if I would rest my head at all. After all, the ground was cleaner than Casa d'Clean Chicks. I put my headlamp on, which lit the path beneath my trusty walking boots and I found solace in the fact that the route before me would be level and clearly marked.

I walked underneath the star-filled sky and enjoyed the cool night air. 34.9 km (21.7 miles) later, I arrived in a small village but nothing was open yet. I fell asleep for over 90 minutes while I was sitting on the ground; propped up against a tree. I finally checked into a pension' owned by an older Spanish woman and quickly sought out the bar for lunch.

The bar had a fantastic inexpensive pilgrim menu, so I eagerly claimed my table and ordered. There was only myself and local fireman on his lunch break and he quickly downed six San Miguel beers before my salad even arrived. All the while, I kept thinking that I needed to pray that my pension' didn't catch fire on his watch. Halfway through my salad, two hundred of the finest locals, in this seventy five populated village, came rushing through the bar doors. They were all yelling in Spanish and ordering drinks. I kept thinking and feeling like I was running with the bulls. I honestly felt fear as cigarette-puffing seniors charged the bar, knocking chairs over at my table. It was like a retirement home outing that was visiting a crack house. As quickly as they came, their three to four drinks were consumed, gossip was shared and the wave of annoying hornets passed. The bar returned to peace but I felt like I had been hit by a Mack truck of old men. I finished my meal in peace, hit the super Mercado for dinner items and hit the bed. No wifi anywhere; what a shocker. Slept all afternoon, through dinner and woke up at 8 a.m. the next morning. The **BIG** walk continues but no small talk desired.

CHAPTER 57

Arrived to Burgos, Spain and spent three hours in hot pursuit of wifi. Spent thirty minutes skyping with Tom and the kids; Lindsay was struggling in Germany and I ended up missing the bus that I was going to cheat with. I ran to end up just watching the bus pull away. No busses. I'm supposed to be walking this! No shortcuts I guess, so I just laughed at the thought and put boot to trail.

Miles later, many miles resulted in all hostels being full. I stopped at a stream to drink and soak my feet; I drank first! I changed into sandals and walked another 3 kilometers to another small village. When I arrived, the hostels refused to accept me because I wasn't wearing boots and they accused me of taking a taxi. The Korean couple quickly stood up for me, stating that they walked with me but the hostel owners rejected me anyway. I was livid! I had walked over 42 miles that day and was exhausted, sore and ravenously hungry. I was so angry and tired; to the point of shaking. I had proof of my stamps along the way but I was still denied.

I started walking, crying and cussing out loud to the sheep, cows and horses but got nowhere for 2.5 km. I turned a corner to see a beautiful brand new hotel. I prepared myself for a "full" sign or paying 100 euros but gleefully paid the asked price of 22 euro; which included wifi, dinner and a private room with bath. Thank you, Jesus! And sorry for the bad words spoken even though nobody else was around to hear. You heard!

Without a sip of water, I dropped my gear in the room, and asked the hotel desk to call me a taxi. I rode back to the prior village hostels and gave them a piece of my mind. I was over the top upset because that was nearly 50 miles of hard walking in 100+ degree weather; only to be judged and turned away. They didn't care and treated me like I was nobody. Other pilgrims approached me outside and said they had been turned away also and asked where I found a room. I gave them all a ride back to my hotel and the taxi driver refused payment, saying that "American Senora is loco and has balls." We all laughed so hard, high-fived and we ate dinner together after they checked in. I drank 4.5 liters of water over ice, skyped with Tom and "Jonathan" for three hours and prepared for bed.

As I was showering, I noticed my shoulders were bleeding. When I checked in the mirror, both shoulders were bloody, bruised and severely swollen. I tended to them and went out and bought maxi pads to put underneath my backpack straps the next day.

The next few days were filled with small villages and I seemed to be back into a part of Spain where redheads were prostitutes. I felt stressed over "Lindsay's" behavior, the lack of "Jonathan's" patience and the pressure to find wifi; my attitude was crap... comprende'? I hated Spain at this point and wanted to get out of that part of the country. I thought about taking a taxi to a special UNESCO site, off of the Camino, but when I checked the pricing with the taxi driver, he said it was 75 euro. I laughed at the absurdity of it and wondered what the prostitute discount was. I found a hostel, ate dinner and was in bed asleep by 5:30 p.m.

I awoke at 3 a.m. and already being dressed for the day, grabbed my boots and gear and snuck out the door, while everyone was sleeping. Another night of walking in the dark! I just love this time by myself. I walked with two people from Berlin after breakfast. Kimber was a quiet 20ish year old girl and Tomratz was a 42 year old man. He we loud, demonstrative and flipped his shoulder-length hair as if he were swatting flies from his eyes; attempting sexy I think. We laughed, walked and made small talk for over 24 km and my spirits began to lift. They were nice and positive in spite of Kimber's feet being full of blisters and Tomratz's obvious pains. I felt the frustrations, anger and negativity begin to lift from my shoulders and somehow the backpack felt lighter; even though I knew that it wasn't. It was 8 km before the next village; the heavens opened up and began a horrific downpour. We continued on for another 3 km until out of the blue the taxi driver from the night before, pulled up and offered us a fare. Five euro for 5 km and 3 people that's a deal so we all thought about it hard, for nearly 1.2 seconds and as we rushed to dump our gear in his large Mercedes trunk, I was told to sit in the front seat; which I did. The five-minute drive turned into a thirty-minute drive as the 75 year-old driver took us around to see all of the sites. As he turned to look at them in the back, his arm or hand kept brushing and bumping against my left breast. Thinking the old man must have a depth of field problem, I ignored this, only to find him rubbing my back as I took a picture of an ancient monument off of the Camino path. Finally the ride came to an end and my friends shook his hand to thank him while passing their cash his way. Feeling I should do the same, he grabbed my hand hard and drew me close to him and gave me a firm hug and kissed my cheek. I pulled away and got angry. He protested saying, "Prostituta."

Tomratz yelled, "No prostitute."

I said, "Si prostitute... 1,000 euro for hug and kiss." The old man yelled something in Spanish and the three of us laughed our heads off as we walked away. It felt so empowering to turn it around and have something to laugh about. We found our way to an albergue' for the night, ate dinner together and by the time I woke in the morning, they were both gone. We never saw each other again but the laughs remain with me to this day. I was in hot pursuit of reaching Leon, Spain and gave myself three days to get there.

CHAPTER 58

Getting to Leon was a long journey filled with many beautiful sights and sites. Once again I found myself walking alone and many times walking during the night. One morning I found myself bored as the wheat fields passed, one after the other, until I came over a hill to see the most beautiful lavender fields. The fragrance filled the air and the sight was almost too much to behold. I stood in awe as I began to breathe deeply and decided to take pictures and then sit in it for a morning picnic. The beauty was incredible and if I close my eyes right now, I can still smell the fragrant breezes. A lovely moment; to say the least and within several kilometers walk, I crested a hill to see a valley of sunflowers. It was a happy sight to me and made me smile.

I arrived in Leon, checked into a hostel with a private room and bath, excited to shower and get some rest. After a few hours of rest, I headed out for the Leon Cathedral. It's a French-style Gothic cathedral started in the thirteenth century over the ruins of the ancient baths, but wasn't completed until the nineteenth century. I found a tiny little sidewalk café at the base of the cathedral and ordered dinner. I used my iPad to videotape the lights illuminating the cathedral at dusk and since the cafe had wifi, I immediately downloaded the video onto Facebook for everyone to see in nearly real time. I was astounded at the following I had created with this big walk and I felt a sense of duty to share each special experience with everyone I knew. Within minutes, the streets, teeming with tourists, became barren and I was alone! I gasped and my first thought was the rapture had occurred and I got left behind; it happened so quickly and there were so many people. I quickly checked my heart with God as I hastily ran in the cold night, making sure not to trip on my flip flops as they hit the stone streets. An older couple sitting at a street café sipping coffee began to laugh at me as I was wearing shorts and squealing from the cold air. They were wearing leather coats and all I could say in my quivering voice was, "Go Camino de Santiago," which made us all laugh even harder, as I was sure to not break my fast stride.

The milestones that I had set on my way to the Cathedral were now dismantled and taken indoors for the night, which caused me to be a bit unsure of my way. The streets were dark, empty and cold as I frantically made my way through the narrow city streets to my hostel. I kept thinking, horror movies start like this. Safely in my room, a little giggle, a sigh of relief and two seconds to strip off my sweaty clothes resulted in a skype call with Tom; from the shoulders up. Slept hard and awoke with a vengeance, ready to move on. As I was walking out of Leon, I ran across the young woman from California that I met a couple of weeks ago. She was cocky and competitive about finishing the walk fast, only to hear her share with me that she quit the very next day after meeting me. This shocked me but I just showed her love, acceptance and was equally surprised when she asked me to pray with her. I did so and continue to do so, on a regular basis. We parted ways with a hug and my BIG walk continued!

Every village I encountered, presented the same red hair issue, but the larger cities were way too busy for my desire and quest for peace. So the next few days were filled with long hours of walking, many kilometers of mountainous terrain and beautiful sights. The peace I so eagerly sought was paid for with severe soreness, pain, bruises, abrasions, broken blood vessels, burnt skin, bug bites and heavy euro. My attitude remained positive and any negatives that I encountered just fueled me to be more loving and helpful to my fellow pilgrims and villagers.

It wasn't long before the redhead issue passed and all people became very kind and loving to me. The whole energy changed on the Camino and my peace had returned. I walked with a smile on my face, my audio Bible playing in one ear, nature in my other ear and a song in my heart.

Many days passed, filled with kind people, pilgrims helping one another, loving Camino workers and amazing scenery. However, I continued running into the family of self-righteous, abusive ministers from my home town and they seemed as frustrated to keep seeing me as I was seeing them! I found myself walking exorbitant amounts of miles, just to avoid them, due to their attitudes; only to walk into a town and see them walking off of a bus at the bus stop. They were bus hopping! Argh, and I still couldn't shake them.

I finally arrived at one of the most sacred sites on the Camino de Santiago... La Cruz de Ferro. It is an amazing and special place with an iron cross that is buried in a massive mound of stones.

Cruce de Ferro ("The Iron Cross" - A Tall Wooden Pole with a metal cross mounted on top and surrounded by millions of pilgrim stones)
Location: The highest point on the Camino,
just outside of Foncebadon Spain

These stones are from the pilgrims. Each pilgrim customarily carries one stone that they brought from home, with a rubber banded prayer around it and they lay it at the cross; symbolizing leaving behind the burdens that you carry in your life. For me, this was an extremely powerful emotional experience.

You see, I had carried 11 stones from home, each with a specific prayer attached and each night before going to bed, I would bring each stone out of my backpack and pray for the person it represented. For, some of the stones represented those that had significantly hurt and betrayed me. By the time I had gotten to the monument, I was no longer angry or bitter at them; rather leaving them and their wrongdoing at the foot of the cross. The weight of these stones that I had carried, in my backpack, had been significant and that's exactly what they had been, heavy weights I had been carrying on my shoulders for so long! The moment I began to take the first one out and read the prayer out loud, I began to cry. I rewrapped the stone and tossed it onto the pile; moving on to the next one and so forth. The tears became heavier as the backpack became lighter! When I was finished, I sat at the base of the monument and just sobbed. Six pounds of stones… sadness… bitterness… grudges… anger… disappointment… despair… frustration… betrayal… ALL left at the foot of the cross. I began to verbally unravel a stream of heartache and I didn't have enough stones for all that I had to say; until I was exhausted and spent. I sat down in the dirt path and sat sobbing in front of everyone. Pilgrims walked up and touched my back or my head. I even had some sit down and pray for me out loud. Everyone was crying as they were going through the same experience. I had chosen to carry so many stones because I had so much hurt and so many that had hurt me! I gathered myself together, picked up my now 36 pound backpack and felt like I could sling it overhead with ease. I prayed as I walked away; thanking God for letting me cast my burdens upon Him. I felt free. I had already become a child of the King but this was different. It was such a visual experience, a powerful thing that changed my life... forever.

Within an hour, I quickly realized that there were other people who I needed to carry a stone for and decided to continue this ritual until Santiago; at that point I would leave the stones there in the Cathedral if possible. I picked up 14 more stones and wrapped them in prayers and took them out nightly to pray over them. Today was a big day and I was weak at every level. Ate like I was starving and slept like I hadn't slept in weeks.

Up and began walking at 3 a.m. Too many places to go and sights to see and I wanted to be with just me and God! The stars were amazing, the air was cool, the bugs weren't biting and the moon was so incredibly big and bright that I didn't even need my headlamp. I'm on a mission now! I have to break the belief barrier for myself, my family, others and many that will read this and yet I may never know their names.

CHAPTER 59

Never spending more than one night in one place, my journey continued with daily hurdles and daily victories! I was achieving HUGE accomplishments by breaking it down into daily goals. By not staying in one place for more than one night, I kept focused on the next goal instead of living in the past; resting on yesterday's victory. Body pains, fatigue and negative pilgrims faced me daily but keeping my head and heart straight, helped me to help others along the way. A good rule of thumb that I reminded myself of daily: Don't "waller" in your failures or revel in your victories for long; for they will both steal the possibilities of your "NOW moments".

I found myself arriving in Sarria, which was 100 km (62.2 miles) away from Santiago. This small city was a starting point for many pilgrims walking to Santiago. In the Catholic Church, pilgrims who walked at least 100 km to Santiago would qualify for the official compostella document and this was supposed to allow a priest to pardon them of their sins. With that in mind, busses and trains were chock full of pilgrims starting in Sarria; many very cocky and dressed in their finest. There were also many large tour groups of people starting here, so as to reap the benefits at the cathedral in Santiago. It was obvious that I had been walking a long distance and many would ask how far and how long I'd been walking, only to have me reply with, "A very long distance." I am not competitive and refused to engage in that behavior…

I walked from Sarria into Portomarin that day and the walk was glorious; although all day was in freezing rain. It was a 22.4 km walk over high and steep mountains but the vistas were well worth the price. The weather was cool, since I was in a higher altitude, so there were no biting insects and pilgrims were in fine moods. I walked into the city over a huge bridge that covered a gorge below which held a fast running river. It was gorgeous and pictures were a must. I quickly found my reserved hostel, grabbed a bottom bunk and started skyping with Tom. Within minutes a Spanish-speaking couple entered the room and began to put their gear up and claim their bunks. She was much younger than he so I made a gross assumption that they were father and daughter. NOT! Two seconds into the room and the young woman strips off clean and begins to grab her shower items. I started to laugh and Tom asked me what was so funny. I had my ear plugs in so they couldn't hear our conversation but it got really funny really fast; especially when the old man began to strip off right in front of me. I said "Senior no!" and he made some crazy hand gestures so I just turned my iPad around and said, "Ola You-tube and skype."

He said, "No, no, no," and grabbed his underroos and covered himself. Tom was laughing hysterically and my virgin eyes were spared! Some sights I could have been spared from but the laughs lasted for hours.

During the rest of my call with Tom, another Spanish-speaking man entered the room and claimed the other bottom bunk next to me. He just sat and listened as Tom and I were talking about our son Michael and his new appointment as an attorney. The next thing I know, he interrupts the conversation to say that he was from the same town and his aunt worked at the university law library. Wow; it's a small world. He seemed like a nice guy so once the call was over, he asked me if I'd like to join him for dinner as many pilgrims do, so I agreed and we were off.

Dinner started off benign but within 30 minutes, this pilgrim opened up and dumped intimate details of his life. He shared that he was bi-polar with psychosis; scaring the bejesus out of me. He shared that he had just come from Israel where he was arrested for telling guards that he had a bomb strapped to his body and was going to blow the bus up. If I didn't hear the rest it was because my head was stuck on the former. He went on to say that he came on the Camino de Santiago to see God and if God doesn't reveal himself to him within the next three days, he was going to blow the Cathedral in Santiago up when he got there. REALLY? Why God? I had a heart to heart discussion of God's love and told him that God was revealing himself right here in me, so he didn't have to blow anything up; I was showing him love, compassion, mercy and acceptance. He kept telling me that God put us together and that we would have to stay together from now on. This guy was totally giving me the creeps and he didn't buy any of my Godly encouragement, so after a three hour dinner and hearing every sordid detail of his past and present, I attempted to change albergues'; only to find that every spot in town was full. I re-entered the bunk bed room to see that the older man and the younger woman were lying on the same bunk; stark nekked! My goodness, I needed me some Jesus! I bid the man from dinner a "Buen Camino," locked and jury-rigged my gear to the bunk bed because I had a bad feeling about this guy and drifted off to sleep. Tomorrow was a new day but I would need to talk with the police about this man; if I didn't and something happened, I would have trouble living with that.

CHAPTER 60

In an attempt to appear to out sleep this man, I was consciously lying in bed, hoping he would leave, when the Spanish couple left. He didn't so I lay there, when all of a sudden I felt my rigged gear shift, so I rapidly flipped over and through squinted eyes, saw the American man trying to get into where my money bag was normally kept. As I flipped over, he jolted and acted like he was fixing the curtains. I waited five minutes as he slipped back in his bed. I jumped up and began lacing my boots, when the Spanish couple returned, and they were appearing to look for something. She pulled money out and acted like she lost some, so I helped her look but she was so upset so with my iPad and the help of an online translator, she said that it was stolen.

Immediately, opened my money sack and showed her what I had and she was satisfied that I didn't have her denominations that were taken. I immediately felt the American had taken it so I told her to wake him. In Spanish, he grossly protested but his face said guilty. I saw him trying to get into my bag and I just knew that he had done it but had no proof. I kept quiet, grabbed my gear and bolted. I found a restaurant open and went for breakfast; staying there for a while in hopes of avoiding this guy. As I paid my bill and prepared to leave, in walked the American. I was shocked, said hello and wished him a Buen Camino. He asked if he could join me on my walk and I politely said that I really wanted to walk alone today so as to contemplate life. He snidely replied, "Well I hope you get there safely and in one piece". What did he mean by that? I had tried to contact police regarding his statements but the business owner said it would be the next day before police would be back in town, so my travels continue.

I needed to avoid this guy so I bolted! I had to make great time and get a head start on him so I made tracks for the bridge. I jumped on the Camino path and it ran straight up on a loose dirt path. The air was thin, breezes were cold and my heart was pumping. I got to the top of the mountain and looked back to see the bridge; only to see him in his neon yellow shirt crossing the bridge coming my way. I began to run! There weren't any other pilgrims around so I needed to move fast! I kept telling myself not to get worked up into a lather but stay calm and run fast. I turned around and saw him at the bottom of the hill and he began to run. I was now scared! Full of adrenaline, I chose to take the paved roadway versus the dirt path because I thought it might deter him from doing anything stupid. I also thought I might be able to flag down a car if I needed to so I kept running and running with my heavy backpack and sore legs.

I checked into a private pension', told them what was going on and they called the police and agreed to tell him I wasn't there. I hid out in the private bedroom and the next day was told that the man stopped 12 km earlier due to blisters. Whew, I had out walked him or should I say out ran him!

I walked another long day throughout the beautiful eucalyptus forests, enjoying the splendid aroma carried on the wings of each breeze and yet staying vigilant about my surroundings. I walked 20 km to another little village and a private pension'. I checked in and told them about the man, only to be told that a man with that name was arrested earlier that morning for threatening to blow up a bar for not serving him beer at 7 a.m. He became violent and found himself in custody. Had a long overdue date with Nair, I got a great night sleep and was back on my way to Santiago. Thank you, God for your many blessings! I sure miss Tom and the children but I know that I need this and they will in turn benefit also. God, please be with them!

Day 24, July 17, 2012. I arrived in Palas de Rei only to have received a message from my sister stating that my father's surgery was delayed because he had suffered a stroke while waiting to go to surgery. Not knowing any further details, the rest of the day was spent sitting on Facebook waiting for an update, researching plane fare to Chicago and trying to contact Tom and the children. I waited 5 ½ hours when word came that Dad was okay. It had been a mild stroke and he was already back to normal. Skyped with Tom and the kids and finally have the answers and peace that I needed. I talked with Dad and he insisted that I continue my walk. After all, I was only 50 km (31.1 miles) from Santiago! I told Dad that I was going to walk the last 50 km's for him and in honor of him! He tearfully thanked me and we parted with I love yous. I couldn't get any medical status information from the hospital staff because my sister didn't give them my name and didn't give me a patient number on him. I felt frustrated that I was so far from him and couldn't get first hand information from those who were giving him medical care but this was par for the course with her.

I awoke after a peaceful night sleep and left town after a great breakfast. Today was going to be an amazing day filled with kind people, beautiful landscapes, good food and walking! Here's for you, Daddy, the last 50 km.

CHAPTER 61

I walked 22 km today through the mountains, sheep poo, mud and flooded waterways that covered the Camino paths. Old stone bridges over creeks, miles upon miles of hand built stone fences, pastures of sheep grazing, sheep bells echoing throughout the hills and friendly villagers handing us water as we passed their doorways. Today was a beautiful walk. I came to a small ice cold spring fed mountain river running through a village and underneath a stone medieval bridge. I found a pension' which had been built in an old stone barn right on that river, so I checked in and quickly changed into my swimsuit and went for a dip. The ice cold water was ridiculously refreshing and I was in heaven. I did my daily duty of washing out my days clothes by hand, hang to dry, showered and went to dinner.

I was enjoying dinner by myself but the next table was occupied by two local sheep herders who seemed to take a fancy to me. They became drunk and began singing very loudly and then began serenading me during my dinner. One dropped to his knees and asked me to marry him. The power of whiskey! There were at least 50 other pilgrims present and everyone was watching, laughing and even joining in on the serenade. Although I found it funny, I also wanted to crawl underneath the table. Said my good-byes, denied the proposal at hand and headed off to get another peaceful night sleep.

The next day's walk was incredibly beautiful. Cool air, precious sights and ended the day with a private pension' that was modern, clean and had great food, at great prices. Another oasis. I cannot believe that I have finally unwound. It's taken me 2 ½ weeks to stop crying and being so emotionally upset. Between "Lindsay's" antics, the French schizophrenic boy that I had to leave, and the body pain; I've had constant tears. There is no doubt that my body severely rejects stress and I must listen and respect that! I spent the evening watching past Army Wives episodes and begin making a list of lessons learned from my journey thus far.

Another great night of sleep and another great breakfast on the Camino de Santiago; I paid my bill and prepared to depart. I was full of vigor and began walking with a group of Swiss older folks who also spoke English. It was a lovely morning with beautiful views and weather. Conversations, as we made our way, were interesting – great small talk. After close to 3 km, the tendon in the back of my left knee began to seriously hurt! One of the Swiss men was a retired doctor, so he taped my knee and told me to walk on the paved road vs. the uneven pathway; so I did. We set a place to meet up for lunch so we split and after

2 km, a car pulled up and out flies the owner of the pension' I stayed in last night and he tells me that I forgot to pay for my bill. That was not the case and I clearly told him that I paid his wife this morning before leaving and did so in front of the Swiss group. He insisted that I pay him and he became indignant. I insisted that I paid his wife so he could just go and talk to her or call the police right now. I was angry about his accusations. I demanded that he phone the police, but he backed down and I told him where I was meeting the group, that they had witnessed my paying her. He got angry and left.

I met up with the Swiss group and when I told them what had happened, they shared that he caught up with them too and accused them of the very same thing. The only thing we could come up with was that there was a communication gap between he and his wife, she was snagging some of that money or this was some kind of racket he had going on. We wondered how many times this has happened and how many times he had gotten away with it because pilgrims got intimidated; therefore just paid the extra! A wonderful memory was marred by greediness, unkind words and attempted theft.

The Swiss group stopped for the night in San Payo for mass but I continued on to Labacolla. There I tended to my painful knee with stretching and ice; then stayed for the night due to the pain. Only 5 km tomorrow until I reach San Marcos; then another 5 km onto the finish line of Santiago! I'll be arriving into Santiago one day earlier than planned, so plan on staying in a pension' for cheap and get my official credential early. I am *so* incredibly excited! I don't want to miss anything in Santiago since it's the huge celebration of the birthday of Saint James.

At dinner, I met a young Iraqi war veteran with a prosthetic leg, who was mountain-biking the Camino alone! He was an amazing young man who wasn't letting any emotional, mental or physical baggage, weigh him down and stop him. We became quick friends and I found myself just mesmerized by his stories and the demonstrative manner in which he shared them. I spent the evening talking with him in great depth, and went to bed with a real sense of inspiration.

I ate breakfast with Tucker and the young teens from Madrid. Tuck biked off and the five of us began our walk together. Beautiful cool day and the walk went fast. We came to the pilgrim cross fence and behind that was my first glimpse of Santiago. Through tear-filled eyes, I began to weave my twig cross into the chain link fence and stood back to view my handiwork. There had to be 2,000 crosses woven into the fence and tears dripped from my lashes as I thought of the many more millions of pilgrims who had crossed this way; over thousands of years.

CHAPTER 62

Shortly after that, we saw Tucker being taken away by ambulance as his bike had been nipped by a passing car; causing his total loss of control over his bike. The villagers were fixing his bike, and putting him up for the night, since he seemed to only have scratches and bruises; no major damage to him at their first evaluation. We were all crying and holding hands in prayerful thoughts but Tucker just smiled and said; come on, toughen up soldiers. Without knowing what the outcome would be, Tucker and I made a pact to meet at the Cathedral de Santiago at 10 am; whether it was tomorrow, the next day or the next day. I would be there every morning at 10 a.m. and would wait for him. I wanted to take his picture in front of the cathedral! We hugged and the Madrid kids and I continued our journey to San Marcos.

I had the idea of ripping open my white pillow case and use it to make a banner for Tucker to see during his next day's trip to Santiago. We all made it, signed our names and strung it between a fence and tree, so that Tucker would feel encouraged during the last stretch to Santiago. What fun and the kids from Madrid were great. We made it to San Marcos Albergue' and took some pretty neat pictures; while standing underneath the monument, which commemorates the visit of Pope John Paul II's visit. This is atop Mount Joy (Monte do Gozo) and the views of the sprawling Santiago suburbs were amazingly exciting!

My knee was killing me but I was almost to the finish line. It's times like these that people quit, slow down, use things as excuses and don't follow through, but I was done and would soon be DONE! I checked into the albergue' for the night and Marco; the man who ran it, was crazy! He spoke 17 different languages and held conversations with every nationality that registered. He was awed by my red hair and asked if he could touch it. He registered my info into the computer and then asked if he could touch it again. Everyone just laughed. He told everyone to be quiet and give reverence; true redheads were sacred. I quietly held thoughts that would shock most. Wow, five days ago, my red hair made me a pariah and today, I am sacred? Spain is muy loco, but I just laughed while going into the kitchen to get ice for my knee.

I had to find my backpack because I had it transported to this albergue' due to my knee not being able to handle the heavy weight and it wasn't here. Marco was excited to lend his expertise to the situation and immediately made everyone wait while he loaded me into his car and drove me up the mountain to a tiny café that had my gear. He asked me if I was hungry and when I said yes, he whipped his car around and took me to the best little café ever. He dropped me off, introduced me to the owner and I was taken care of like a queen. Marco said he had to return and finish the pilgrims but would return quickly. Within 15 minutes, he was back and having dinner with me. Marco was a kind middle-aged man, who was quite inquisitive and without restraint asked many prying questions. He was harmless and I loved the childlike mindset and yet the responsible nature of his personality. If I could have only brought him home with me I would have. I know two or three super women that he'd love to meet; match-making on the Camino de Santiago. Wow; it pays to be a redhead in Galicia, Spain.

Washed out my clothes, iced the knee again and went outside to rest in the grass. While there, I met two amazing young women, both with incredible stories of their own. Christine was 18 years old and was a cancer survivor from Philly; walking by herself. We instantly bonded as I saw much of myself in her. Walking the Camino de Santiago was her lifelong dream and according to her, the Make A Wish Foundation had paid for everything for her to be able to make that dream come true. Then there was Heather from Toronto. She was a middle aged lady whose husband was killed just a couple of weeks earlier while cycling together. The driver had fallen asleep at the wheel, hitting her husband and he died in Heather's arms. She is a successful attorney and business woman, but at that moment, she was a broken little girl who was lost and hurting. I spoke to them as if God were talking through my vocal chords. Words I couldn't have imagined coming up with just slipped from my lips and it was pure love. I prayed with each of them and then we finished a prayer in a group; arms interlocking and tears falling from their cheeks. By the time I looked up, the group of 3 had grown into a group of almost 30 pilgrims. I was just speaking from my heart to theirs, but God wanted other hearts to hear too… I continue to pray for each of them daily; wherever they may be… God is with them both!

I lay in bed, knowing it was my last night on the Camino de Santiago and silently wept. I didn't want it to be over. One small blister, a super sore knee, consistent body aches, but that was normal for the level of workout I was experiencing, and a heart that was being healed. I gave myself three months to do it and will be completing it in 30 days! I am only 5 km from Santiago, the last 50 km for Daddy.

CHAPTER 63

I woke early and laced my boots with a passion. Five km to go and I will have crossed the finish line into Santiago! I am *so* excited! I am acutely aware of the finality that each step taken presents and I am filled with a melange of emotions. The kilometers pass quickly and every step taken goes downhill, so it's done with ease.

At 9:22 a.m. July 23, 2012 I rounded the narrow street in Santiago, Spain; seeing the cathedral peek its gorgeous Romanesque spirals through the gap in the horizon. ***I DID IT !*** I stood before the Cathedral dumbfounded. Not sure what to feel and yet I felt so much. A lot of tourists were taking pictures of a handful of pilgrims who had arrived. I, with my backpack gear, skort, hiking boots and poles, just stood there with my mouth gaping, until I heard a man ask me if he could take my picture. I said yes, thank you and then I left to go find my albergue' for the night. I anticipated that my finishing the walk would result in my dramatically falling to my knees and kissing the Cathedral courtyard, but nothing. No emotion really; just another accomplishment but I felt great! I found my albergue' and got my gear settled, took a shower and headed back to the Cathedral. By this time it was 10 a.m. sharp, so I sat and waited for Tucker to arrive.

At 11:22 a.m. Tucker rode into the Cathedral Plaza and it was truly beautiful! We cheered, cried and I took lots of pictures for him. When he first saw me waiting for him in the plaza, he cried like a little boy and thanked me for the banner. He said that he knew it was me and he couldn't thank me enough for the act of support. I told him the Madrid kids helped and he smiled ear to ear. He turned around and the banner was hanging from his backpack like a war flag! He was so adorable, as he held up his bike over his head, while standing in front of the Cathedral. While the sun was glistening off of his prosthetic leg, I got some good pictures and we were both so obviously proud of each other. What an amazing young man of strength, fortitude, stamina, inspiration and persistence. Biking 500 miles, through the French Pyrenees by himself and with a prosthetic leg; my Iraqi War veteran friend had done it. The power of the human spirit, the will to not give up in the face of what appears to be an insurmountable obstacle, loss, hardships, devastation and grief! This **BIG WALK** filled with small talk, has changed my walk through life! I will never be the same.

Tucker stayed for mass, so we said our good-byes, since his flight for the US was leaving at 4:00 p.m. After departing,

I realized we didn't get any pictures together; ugh! I will never forget Tucker.

I will rest today, buy something suitable to wear to mass tomorrow and see some sights. Tomorrow morning I will get my official compostella and enter the Cathedral for the very first time – it's going to be a huge Pilgrim mass at noon. I was exhausted yet invigorated, sad but excited. God is good!

I returned to my albergue' and was greeted by this sweet little Spanish speaking older woman dressed in a full length black dress and crying. I asked her if she was okay and she just cried harder. I wrapped my arms around her and guided her to a chair in the dining area. She was the owner and started to tell me that her husband had died twelve days before and that she was so incredibly sad. She told me that the government had already sent her a letter asking her for money on behalf of her husband and said it was in English; if I could please read it to her. I agreed and held her hand while she cried. She thanked me for my kindness and said that I looked like an angel with the sunlight shining through my beautiful red hair. I giggle and thanked her for her sweet words. I couldn't help but thinking of the heartache I had endured regarding this red hair but now I was being rewarded for not quitting. The kind words and compliments would continue throughout the rest of my stay in Santiago.

I decided that I would go to the official office to get my Compostella document of the Camino de Santiago completion.

After waiting in line for over 2 ½ hours, having 7 pilgrims rejected for fraudulent claims of completion, my emotions began to well up from deep within me. I approached the desk and was asked for my US Passport and my Pilgrim Passport of stamps. I was then asked if I walked the whole way and I said yes. Then I was asked where my journey began and I told them Paris but a train was taken to St Jean Pied de Port. The man carefully examined my passport of stamps, asked me a few more questions and as he congratulated me, I burst into tears. In front of everyone waiting in line and all of the workers, I was in tears. I DID IT! An obese, middle-aged, inactive woman with a brain tumor... walked 800+ km (500+ miles) through horrific terrain and weather, all by myself! If I can do this, anybody can! My Official Compostella is written in Latin; including my name and is absolutely beautiful. I got my picture taken with the nun who was working the desk and I was on cloud nine. What an amazing feeling.

I was calculating in my approach, in my walk, in my thinking, in whom I walked with, in whom I celebrated with and I DID IT! Now what? I began walking the streets of Santiago for hours after dinner. I ran across a little shop of pedicures with huge tanks of dead skin eating fish and for 20 euro, I got the best pedicure of my life! An amazing and crazy experience that required videotaping and posting on Facebook. What a glorious day.

I was in bed by 9 p.m., for a peaceful night sleep, in my private room only costing 15 euro. The old building and my room had very high ceilings, old plumbing and tall thin French windows that opened out and revealed wrought iron balconies that overlooked a plaza filled with sidewalk cafés and tables with umbrellas. Window boxes teeming with bright colorful cascading flowers and the narrow streets echoed with sounds of street performers, from accordion players to violinists and acoustic guitars. At one point a jazz saxophone player began to wail and I fought to keep my eyes open. I loved this and will never forget the old house, the old woman in mourning, the plaza of music, the smell of amazing food and the cool breeze blowing the thin curtains into the center of my room. Thank you God… for ALL of it.

CHAPTER 64

I awoke after 11 hours of sleep and left for my luxury hotel (San Francisco Hotel Monumento). It was absolutely incredible. It was just 150 short meters from the Cathedral, in the historic center of Santiago de Compostela. It was built in the eighteenth century and was a Franciscan convent but had been turned into a 5 star luxury hotel. This was Tom's gift to me for completing the treacherous BIG WALK! What a gift; as I walked into the lobby to check in, I was walking on clear paneled floors that were elevated over the original stone flooring and was lit up. My room was pure luxury in every way and I was in 5 star heaven! The rooms normally went for over 540 euro which is nearly $700 USD per night but Tom got it for 60 euro per night! Thank you, Tom for your generosity and your belief in me! WIFI and the best part was that the bellboy carried my backpack and gear to my room; I just had to laugh as I handed him 5 euro for doing so and thought how far I'd already carried it. I pulled the floor to 25 foot ceiling curtains back and revealed a set of floor to ceiling glass French doors, that opened out onto a beautiful balcony; overlooking a gorgeous green courtyard below. Birds singing everywhere, butterflies flitting about and the sound of nuns singing in the abbey! What a glorious way to celebrate completing my walk on the Camino de Santiago. Today was going to be the Pilgrim Mass at noon and I hurriedly got ready.

By 10:30 a.m. I entered the Cathedral through the Master Mateo's masterpiece "Door of Glory" for the very first time. Custom has it that the pilgrims entering the Cathedral for the first time, does so on their knees in appreciation and humility for their safe arrival, then place their hand in the "Tree of Jesse" which is the central column of the Doors of Glory. I humbly lowered my head in reverence but I only get on my knees for my God and I've already been humbled before him many times during this journey. This cathedral was built in 1116 and the Bible and main characters come alive in the storybook on stone. The central stone has Christ in all of his glory, surrounded by His apostles and sitting just below them is St. James (as intercessor between Christ and the pilgrim).

I made my way into this massive and spectacular Cathedral; finding a seat that was close to the altar. At 11:55 a.m. the huge door closed and the mass was going to begin. I sat with such anticipation. Although there are seats for 1,000 pilgrims, every seat was taken and the floors were covered with those choosing that option. The mass began and it was beautiful, very reverent, nuns singing like angels, the smells, bells and robed figures. I was awestruck at the passionate belief that goes into the daily discipline required to maintain something like this... how could one not respect that? As the mass continued, six – eight robed attendants (tiraboleiros in Spanish) rose and began to lower the massive Botafumeiro (incense burner). The swinging of the massive incense burner was originally performed to fumigate the sweaty and disease-prone pilgrims where they sat. As the burner was lit, the cathedral became engulfed with a thick smoke and the attendants pulled the long braided cord in unison and the burner began to rise to the ceiling and swing. The burner swung from one end of the cathedral to the other; right over the heads of the pilgrims. It was a truly magnificent sight to see; one that I pray never fades from my memory. As the mass came to a conclusion, I grabbed my place in line so as to see the crypt and final resting place of the Apostle St. James (Disciple of Jesus). The line was lengthy; at least 200+ people waiting but I didn't walk 500+ miles to skip this sight! As my turn came to enter the crypt, there was a kneeling bench for prayer at the tiny opening that revealed his sterling silver resting place. There were two steps between the kneeling bench and the gate to his silver burial site and I put my backpack down, knelt on the bench and took out one stone at a time. I prayed for each person and the tears began to flow. As I finished each prayer, I set the rock, wrapped in its prayer, on the step in front of me and started my own prayer mound. Fourteen stones for fourteen people, that had poured themselves into me, reciprocated and loved me for who I was. These were people that I wanted to surround myself with and pour myself into them. You each know who you are because we have had conversations since and I know that to this day, not only are those fourteen stones still there; more have been added by other pilgrims since. As I was laying down each stone, praying and crying, passers-by that were visiting the crypt, laid their hand on my head and shoulder and many were crying seeing me go through this ritual. Visitors knew exactly what I was doing and most knew the significance of the act. No, I didn't think St. James was acting as intercessor but to me, the act of doing what I did, was symbolic to other pilgrims. I topped the pile of stones with a thin little bracelet that "Lindsay" had given me to wear for the Camino journey; the stones enveloped by the stretch circle of brightly beaded love.

I left the crypt and spent the next four hours sitting in the Cathedral; quietly and reverently. Many thousands of generations of families dedicated their lives to build the cathedrals of the world and yet visitors, in their ignorance, aimlessly meander through the chapels, gawking at the beauty but not understanding the belief and dedication that drove this level of love; generational legacy of service.

Gliding my fingertips along the wooden pews or the ornately carved stone; sent my heart reeling. Listening to the bells and smelling the smells of this massive tribute to God and St. James, was causing a sensory overload for me. Who were you St. James? You've nagged my thoughts for 28 years, calling me to walk the Camino de Santiago and now I've done it. Will your quiet whispers stop or will you bid for my return?

I rejoined the cities celebration of St. James' birthday that evening and ran into one of the twelve who I ate dinner with in St. Jean Pied du Port, the night before I began. He told me that none of the others finished the walk and he hadn't either; informing me that it was just too hard and he was too sore... excuse after excuse. He asked me where I had stopped and when I told him that I had finished it, he didn't believe me and wanted to see my compostella. I took it out of my backpack and he began to speak of his shame and guilt. When I inquired, he said that he'd spent part of his retirement 401K to do it and then didn't finish. He said he felt like a failure. I put my hand on his and said that his walk has really just begun. Every step he will forever take, will be his Camino and every person who crosses his path will be a pilgrim on their walk through life. How he treats them, whether he walks a walk of integrity, love, forgiveness and service is totally up to him and that's a walk that's far more important. I asked him what he learned from walking the Camino de Santiago and he began to share lessons that he received during his weeks walk. His eyes welled up, he thanked me, kissed my cheek and I never saw him again.

I enjoyed dinner overlooking the Cathedral and the plaza began to fill up with thousands of people. That night was the celebratory light show and concert on the side of the Cathedral. Not sure what to expect, I decided to stay in spite of the sardine cramped plaza filled with Spaniards that must have eaten too many beans that day. The light show was beyond spectacular and I am so glad that I stayed. It was amazing and well worth the 8 hour wait, standing in the Plaza. Brilliant display of lights and music; all geared towards telling the story of St. James' journey from Jerusalem and how Santiago de Compostella came about. A night filled with pure magic; to say the least.

My last day in Santiago was filled with great food, jacuzzi soaks, swimming in the pool house for hours, relaxing in the sun and meeting a friend of "Jonathan's" from Germany. Her name was Mara and she was a sweet girl who happened to be there that week for school. She was a lovely high-spirited girl who insisted on walking me all over the city on a guided tour of everything I'd already seen. Needing to walk anyway and not wanting to spoil the sharing of her new Santiago knowledge, I walked, listened and appeased. We parted and I ate dinner at the Cathedral Square and skyped Tom and the kids. Thank you God and Tom!

The next day I left Santiago. As my plane was leaving the airspace over Santiago, I couldn't stop crying. I didn't want it to end. I knew that this time of my life was special and I genuinely didn't want it to end... then I was reminded of the words I had spoken to the other pilgrim about his walk. I have walked through HELL... the hell of my childhood, my college years, my early adult life and the hell of this horrific terrain and weather, all of the while looking at heaven! I chose to finish the journey that I was called to do and yes, there was a price to pay, consequences and rewards. In attempting greatness, many lost their lives, many quit when things got difficult, many made excuses but the few who finished had achieved greatness! Each person must walk their own journey… and reap what they sow.

I gave myself three months to walk it and I did it in ONE! Now what? Off to Germany to meet up with the children and then? I was a different person. My walk had truly just begun…

PART 6

BIG WALK…
BIG TALK !

CHAPTER 65

Now you know what brought me to the walk and what got me THROUGH the walk… There are many lessons learned, parallels drawn and insights gained from that BIG WALK. Now it's time to talk! Parallels were seen that cross the lines of business, personal, family, spiritual and relationally. Lessons, parallels and insights that I hope will provoke your thoughts and cause you to dig deep into your emotions. I am calling for a thought revival!

The first parallel that I experienced, during this journey, was the path in general. I have had many difficult times throughout my life; just as the path terrain and weather were equally uneven, treacherous and unpredictable. The path was filled with freezing rain, mud, excessive high temps, sheep poo, valleys, steep mountaintops, rocky, narrow, dangerous spots and even deadly places; just as our walk through life is. Getting to the top isn't easy but you cannot talk your way up the mountain; you must walk up! Every journey of success is filled with peaks and valleys, rough spots, aches, pains, tears, laughter, little failures and little victories, that all lead us to the final destination... success!

Did I feel fear? Absolutely! I remember standing at the starting line and looking straight up, at the first of the French Pyrenees Mountains, and feeling pure unadulterated terror running through my veins! But I had two choices... FEAR = FORGET EVERYTHING AND RUN or FACE EVERYTHING AND RISE! It's a choice we all face in our lives. What is our first instinct? What choice do we finally make? For some, they quit right there and then. They use everything and anything as an excuse; rather than using those as reasons for plunging forth, pushing into and having victory. They have a blister, sore legs, started their monthly cycle, can't afford it, they're lonely or their family is missing them too much. I've heard them all. For others, they will experience these issues and they turn those into reasons! "I must complete this goal for my family; my obstacles will offer a platform to inspire others." We all have issues arise in life but the winners aren't whiners; they aren't those that take exception but who are the exception. Again, it's all a choice.

What would happen, if each person reading this book, were to take personal responsibility for where they are in their life and stop blaming their childhood, parents, bosses, spouses or the mailman? What if they were to take their power back, interrupt the same old patterns of thinking, take a step in another direction and put one foot in front of the other? A different reality would occur, in your life and the lives of those around you.

I felt total fear to step out of the old and into the new, to walk away from the title, status, income and lifestyle that I had created so that I could take my power back and step into greatness, a great new me. I felt total fear as I left my doctors, husband, children and all things familiar behind for a short time, so that we could all have long-term gain. I felt fear as I strapped on a 47 pound backpack filled with stones and unnecessary "needs" and prayed that I wouldn't tip over in front of all of Paris. I felt fear as I left home at a young age and hid out amongst the anonymous of the parks. I felt fear to take a chance and open my heart to love again; worried that my love would be deadly to him too. Most of all, I felt fear of what example I would be setting for my children and those watching if I didn't finish. I felt the fear and chose to face everything so I could rise!

Be brave enough to honestly self-evaluate your childhood messages, patterns and pathology. Be courageous enough to throw your foot over the boat of fear, so you can do the impossible; even if it feels like this faith will lead you to walk into uncharted deep waters. If what you're doing isn't bringing the results you desire, then set the example for those watching and show them how to take a step down a different path; how to change their life. Does it mean you have to take up your cross and walk 2,000 miles through Europe alone? Not necessarily… Change starts with honesty rather than denial.

CHAPTER 66

First call... for honesty. There were many types of pilgrims, as there are in our daily life; which are you?

Pilgrim "Jones": Competitive with others and had to walk the furthest or fastest for the day? Always trying to get one leg up on your neighbor, be the big man, drive the nicest car in the neighborhood, have the best dressed kids and undermine your neighbors' journey in the slightest way, so as to make yourself look better? The pilgrim who had the name brand gear, stayed in all private hotels and made sure everyone knew about it. Walking with a Pilgrim "Jones" either brought out the competitive side of you or a defensive "C.Y.A." attitude. I chose to avoid these types as I had walked from business associates and leaders that were like this, so why would I choose to walk this special journey with them? Life isn't a race; do your own pace but put a demand on your potential.

Pilgrim "Mememe": Focusing solely on their own needs, wants, desires and completely ignoring a fellow pilgrim in need.

Walking past those in obvious pain, without a second thought as to whether or not they might be able to lend a helping hand. Complaining at every meal, every hostel, to every pilgrim they meet along the way because they felt an injustice. Why? Because they were too busy focused on, "Me me me." I chose to avoid these pilgrims because I no longer allowed anyone in my life that was self-serving and self-consumed. This walk would be my first test of this new pattern of thinking!

Pilgrim "Wine": Solely focused on moving from one village to another just so they could taste the wine from that areas vineyards. They were usually tipsy, loud, obnoxious and disturbing to others, before dinner was even served with no regard for others. Partying their way through the "Way" was their focus and I wondered if they would even remember the journey, let alone get anything from it, other than a perpetual hangover. I walked through ten years of life with an alcoholic not even a second thought given to walking on this journey with this pilgrim.

Pilgrim "Whine": Constantly complaining about their aches, pains, blisters, heat, rain, bugs, the sun, the clouds, villagers and of course, whined about how negative other pilgrims were being. Weren't they aware that negativity breeds negativity? We must be careful who we walk through life's journeys with. Walking with a whiner or those with negative attitudes, will only slow you down and make you more aware of your own aches and pains! No thank you! I avoided these pilgrims like they had the plague; not because I was unkind, but rather I loved myself enough to not make it harder on me that needed.

Pilgrim "Dora": Exploring, only in it for the adventure and had no interest in introspection, always grinning at those pilgrims on a heart search and pokes fun at those seeking answers or wise counsel. I found these pilgrims needing to search but too deep in denial to even explore that option.

Pilgrim "Lips": Each evening was spent conversing with other pilgrims, over dinner, about how many times they had walked the Camino or giving advice on short cuts and such. Talked a big game but when others weren't looking, would limp their way to a grassy knoll for rest. I got to a point when I no longer offered an answer when I was asked how many times I'd walked the Camino or where I started. I believe in letting your walking do the talking! My answer became "A while back" and I'd leave it at that. Are you doing more talking than walking? Are you giving your boss, leaders, spouse and friends big lip service without any action behind it? You lose credibility when you keep stating huge goals but do nothing; an act that I call "verbal masturbation".

Pilgrim "Saint": Those pilgrims who are service focused, always willing to lend a hand to those that have fallen, a bandage to the wounded, food to the hungry, water to the thirsty, words of encouragement to those downtrodden and kindness to those in pain. These are pilgrims who tend to be magnets for the needy and confused, but seem to always carry a smile on their face. I enjoyed walking with these pilgrims because they were kind and giving; always appreciative when another pilgrim gives to them first.

Pilgrim "Loner": Always walking alone, withdrawn, detached and unwilling to interact with other pilgrims in any way. These are people who have brick walls up and push others away so as to avoid getting attached and/or hurt. They desire nothing more than a sense of community, acceptance and approval but won't let anyone close enough so as to achieve that. These pilgrims seem very sad and lonely; although there are many opportunities to connect with other pilgrims during their journey. I was called to walk this journey alone, even though I didn't push people away from myself, I certainly had to make a concerted effort to stay true to task. When my path crossed another walker's, I felt that they were placed there by divine guidance, not happenstance. I took each situation as a learning opportunity; leaving with a new awareness.

Pilgrim "Butterfly": Socially flitting from pilgrim to pilgrim as if they were pollinating their way through Spain. There to increase their friends list on social networking sites, these pilgrims did nothing but make small talk and walk. Nothing wrong with this but sometimes peace and quiet does a soul good. There's something to say with someone that never allows any level of deep connection, but only rather superficial exchanges.

Pilgrim "Shovel": These pilgrims would walk with you and dig deep trying to find out your biggest secrets and were relentless to do so. It was almost as if their real quest was to dig up as much dirt as feasibly possibly; although I'm not sure what the gain was in doing so. Deciding to live life with a healthy level of defense, my chain link fence was disarming to this type of pilgrim. Many of them expected either a brick wall or a total open book, I was neither. My fence was slightly giving, I could touch, feel, see and hear the diggers but they weren't able to penetrate the barrier; unless I chose to open the gate and reveal.

Pilgrim "Dump Truck": Brimming with internal muck, these pilgrims were quick to dump their anger, bitterness, sadness, and life's story into your backpack as they walked next to you. A willing ear soon learned that this level of discord effected and affected anyone that chose to share their space.

Pilgrim "Holiness": Talking God and hitting every mass in sight, this type of Pilgrim was doing their best to be holy. Talk righteously, behave spiritually and wear their cross with pride... making sure that every pilgrim they encounter is invited to mass with them. All of this effort and yet don't they know they can't earn their way into God's favor. It's a simple gift; nothing we deserve, or can pay for in word or deed, a gift. Ephesians 2:8-9 KJV, "For by grace are ye saved through faith and that not of yourselves, it is the gift of God: Not of works, lest any man should boast." Am I suggesting that attending church or wearing a cross is wrong?... absolutely not. I just wonder the significance and effectiveness one has for God, when we put fish signs on our cars and then flip the middle finger to those who cut us off in traffic. Does our walk match our talk?

Lastly, Pilgrim "Chi": This person was a calming force of even temperament, choosing to walk alone at times, socializing, sharing and inquiring when appropriate. They were always willing to lend a helping hand, caring ear and supplies, thoroughly enjoying the solitude of nature and pilgrim interaction that St. James brought their way. Keeping a healthy balance and yet making the most of their journey of enlightenment. Others never needed to hear them talk of God because they were walking testaments of God's love. These pilgrims were a joy to walk with, dine with, talk to and share space.

What type of pilgrim are you? What type do you wish to be? What type of pilgrims are you surrounded by at work and in your private life? What type of pilgrim do you attract? Once you have this down, then ask those in your life, that you trust to be honest, what type of pilgrim that they see you as. Honesty and awareness are the first steps to change.

CHAPTER 67

Once you figure out where you are, from the pilgrim lists, then it's time to evaluate your attitude. Do you find yourself complaining a great deal or chronically sounding negative in general, albeit words, thoughts or deeds? The old saying that one's attitude determines one's altitude is absolutely true but I take it a step further. Your altitude will also determine the tone in your home and the attitudes of those around you as well as those who you will continue to attract. Focus on things you're grateful for in your life, having an attitude of gratitude. Find the sunshine in a situation and make sure that this is what you talk about. Possibilities are positive in nature, whereby limitations are negative! What you think about, dream about, talk about and believe you will bring about. Therefore having a negative attitude and having that reflect through words and deeds, only fuels more of the same. Again, this is all within your power to choose! It is a choice!

Once you have in your mind, what personality type you are and what your attitude is you can make changes right here! Decide if this is all working for you! Do you like the outcome of your interactions based on attitude and behavior. Are you attracting success, successful people, possibilities and people with "find a way" attitudes into your life or are you surrounded by naysayers, negative nellies, whiners, takers and talkers? If you don't like the results you are getting or don't like where you are finding yourself, then change it! It all starts with a two second decision for change! Fill in the blank...

I am tired of_____.
I no longer want _____ in my life.
I take personal responsibility for _____.
I am changing _____.
I desire _____ in my life.

Be passionate about your answers, insight and changes that you are committed to! People will try to test you, balk at your decisions and behavioral changes but if you are consistent, they'll eventually get it. Recognize and allow yourself to feel the full breadth of your emotions right now. You may have held these in for years. It's normal and healthy but feeling these hidden emotions begin to bubble up to the surface, will cause many people to stop doing anything or even talking about it. These emotions cannot hurt you unless you hide them away again; feelings buried alive never die! I am putting a demand on your potential right this second. If you don't take steps to be better, you will become or remain bitter! Which will it be? Make a decision right now and sign your name to the bottom of this page as your commitment to become better! Those who do not make this commitment will continue to talk big and walk small! This is it, your time to step into change, embrace it and walk into greatness!

Your Signature as a personal commitment for change !

Today's Date

CHAPTER 68

Once you've made your commitment for change; you are then on your way to becoming a better you and having a better life!

The next step that I took was to dig deep from my gut and find a dream that I had never fulfilled; a goal. Placed and sitting on the back burner, because the timing wasn't right, etc. A dream that had been tucked away and faded with time but still carries a burning ember. Write that goal down on paper. When you see it on paper, do you get a rush?... A queasy stomach?... Goosebumps? A passionate burning, that resides deeply in your chest? If not, keep digging up the dreams peeling them away like layers of an onion, until you find the one that does give you the visceral reactions you're looking for. It might be a dream of changing the types of people you attract, circles of influences, your job environment and so forth. Whatever it is, write it down! You can certainly have more than one! Write it down and then ask yourself why would you want to ever see this dream accomplished? Write it down and keep digging until you get the visceral reaction to the why. There you have it... YOUR DREAM, YOUR GOAL AND YOUR WHY and Date of Completion! Without a final destination (Goal) and a date of completion (TOA – Time of Arrival), then you aren't on a big walk, you're just talking big, but walking small; taking a stroll and that will bring about delayed accomplishments and distractions, that leads to discouragement. This is a vital component for change!

Now you have to have an ACTION PLAN a plan of attacking this goal. Two thousand plus miles walked through Europe! If I didn't have certain things in place, I would have never made it to the finish line. I took my overall goal (800 km) and set a date of completion (3 months). I then broke it down into 5 km segments per day. That was a reasonable goal with a reasonable action plan that would eventually get the goal accomplished but as time passed, I decided to up the daily activity because I didn't like the results. I wanted to get there faster, get through the harder parts quicker, so I bumped it up and went to 10 km per day, then 15 and up to 65 km per day! Shoot for the moon and if you miss, you'll land among the stars! I finished in one month not three! So I took the next two months and traveled through 14 countries throughout Europe; just having fun! My celebration... my reward. So what is your action plan to help you turn that dream into your reality?

Dream: _____

WHY? _____

Goal: _____

Plan of Attack: _____

Date of Completion: _____

Your WHY for Completion?: _____

Once you have set your dream / goal in place, have why, action plan and date of accomplishment the first thing you will feel is a rush of exhilaration but many times that is quickly followed by fear! This is a critical point. It's at this time, most people will Forget Everything And Run! But there will be those who feel the fear and Face Everything And Rise! What have you got to lose? You're not as happy as you could be, you aren't happy with the results your life is bringing forth. Maybe you're not happy with you? Take a chance, a calculated risk for change. Fear will be the first pitfall for many, just step over and through it! It's a choice.

Once you've take the first step through FEAR start getting prepared! Don't skimp on preparations. You'll either pay now or pay later; either way, you'll pay! Decide what are NEEDS and what are WANTS! (Most are wants you know). Streamline your systems so you can work your action plan smoothly, travel lightly and put your energy into activities that will really help you move forward. Painting your bathroom isn't one of them unless your goal is to sell your home and the kids have peeled the paint off of the bathroom walls. I remember buying a product called Nu Skin (a liquid protective coating for wounds etc). This was a must and also a must for you in your quest for dream realization. No, don't go out and buy this unless you need it as a reminder but remember, as you move through your action plan, you might get hurt feelings, bruised knees, elbows and blisters; even others angry at you. Remember, your shifting, shifts them and some people don't like change! When this occurs, imagine opening the Nu Skin product and using the brush to coat over that wound, protecting the tender sore place beneath. This is a powerful visual that will bring you through difficulties and the protective coating will create a thin barrier so as to protect from future hurts.

Prepare your heart and mind! There will be a price to pay for these changes. Know this up front and don't act shell-shocked when it comes to light. You will pay with your time, energy, financial investment, inconvenience, difficulty, obstacles, naysayers, aches, pains, fatigue, wounds, lost rewards, daily goals not always met, friends that quit or distance themselves from you, people that stop supporting and encouraging you! What you will achieve and gain, is change, betterment, accomplishment, success, self-esteem, confidence, insight, new lifestyle filled with new healthy people and self-respect. Preparation is critical but many will stay in this phase. They will train to start, just start! Don't prepare for 10 years or that's 9 ¾ years wasted. Passionately prepare and work your plan on a

CHAPTER 69

You've taken your first step on the path of success and health; whether it's a journey in business, social life, personal, spiritually or even physically. It's all the same and requires effort. Walking the action plan, you will encounter many potholes, danger spots, peaks, valleys, trials and difficulties. I learned many things that might be helpful along your path through change.

Trust the arrows and way markings of those that have gone before you, they know the pitfalls and the right direction; giving you wise counsel. Don't second guess the arrows; the doubt comes from your old "tapes" and messages that had you stuck where you were before.

Be careful whom you choose to walk with as their presence will certainly effect you. Don't let your friends choose you, you choose your friends! Family isn't only determined by DNA; it's a choice. Who will you walk through life with? They will either speed you up, slow you down, effect your attitude, distract you or take you astray.

Watch constantly the ground you walk upon, plus four steps ahead of you; one misstep can result in taking the wrong path, injury or even death, certainly putting an abrupt end to your journey. Stay focused. Distractions result in getting your eyes and attention off of the task at hand, lost, hurt or hurting others. Minimize distractions and have a passionate focus on your why and the finish line!

The middle of your journey is the hardest. It's usually the most difficult because you're tired, sore, discouraged and seems to stretch on forever. Your goal finish line is closer than you think but if you keep looking into the rear view mirror to judge how far you've come, you will not be looking through the windshield to see where you need to go; which is so much more important. That's why the windshield is so much larger than the rear view mirror. It's at this critical point you will be faced with a decision. Do I quit (easier) or do I push into the next stage and push through to success? It's a choice. Nobody will judge you but there is a price to pay for this decision too. Are you ready to walk in your quiet shame and guilt? If not, don't stop; instead, view it as a speed bump and speed up your momentum and efforts! That will push you through this part the fastest. Many quit here. What does it take for you to quit. To give up? A bad day, biting flies, extreme heat, running into someone with a bad attitude, chronic rain, mud, getting off track, losing friends because they quit, seeing others take short cuts or cheat? Getting to the finish line with integrity and character only sweetens the victory! "Nobody would know." You will know! You either live with your proud victories or walk in your shameful failures but ultimately you live with yourself. It's all choices! Will you rationalize, make excuses, justify or will you get recommitted to being better instead of quitting and being bitter? To me, that's the true definition of character.

In your quest to be better, you must make sure to meet your own needs in the process. Sleep when needed, eat healthily, drink lots of water, take frequent breaks to retighten your "boots" or attitudes, surround yourself with positive thinkers, people and motivation. I carried a picture of Santiago de Compostella in my money bag and every time I felt down or discouraged, I'd take it out and reinvigorate myself. When your days purposeful activity is over, lose the boots, kick back, change your shoes and relax. You deserve it and that separate time helps you recover and recharge.

Find a commonality and goal with others and pull together to support, encourage and help one another. Team work; without even realizing it. Random acts of kindness and assistance takes the most people to the finish line if they want it badly enough. You reap what you sow, so sow kindness, love, encouragement, passion, compassion and integrity. If you are "me" focused, then you will miss the joy of learning how to serve. A true leader cannot lead where they aren't willing to go, cannot do what they aren't willing to do and cannot be served until they have mastered the art of learning how to serve.

Confidence comes from repeating a behavior until it's mastered. So, put one foot in front of the other, never give up even if some days are baby steps and take others along with you! Don't stay in one place for too long whether it's reveling in past victories or slouching in your past failures. Feel it, learn from it and move on! Don't stop at the first sign of discomfort or inconvenience, tighten your boots and make a daily recommitment to your goal. Don't sacrifice your health, safety, needs and future for those who don't value their own. Remember, the path gets narrower towards the end because only the few who choose will finish. Many will opt to be cheerleaders, spectators, big talkers, excuse makers or your worst critic, but they won't be there at the finish line because only winners finish! Live simple, travel light, have a passionate purpose, stay focused, inspire others and make a difference in the journeys of others.

CHAPTER 70

So many people had been placed in my path, lessons learned, stories heard, pain endured, as well as tears shed and shared. I was willing to honestly dig deep, do the work, take the risks, allow myself to be vulnerable and the payoff was huge! In turn, my thinking has been stretched, my health restored, healthy friends made, increased self confidence, self worth, self esteem and am no longer in my shell of inadequacy. A higher level of spiritual visual acuity was achieved. I no longer self-sacrificially ignore my needs, am unwilling to take on stress inducing commitment and I am less tolerant for narcissistic demanding people in my life. I now have improved awareness in spotting them before the impending sucking sound of the vacuum begins.

I had walked through hell while looking at heaven, came out on the other side, a new creature, feeling like I've fought my way out of the birthing canal and seeing light for the first time. You have choices to make in your life. You don't have to look like, act like or be like others in order to be successful, loved and loving; just be you and walk. What do you want to attract in your life! Funny, but soon others will aspire to be like you.

It doesn't matter what your past held and your future is relative to today! Make today count. Your future will be molded not by your past but by what you do today and every day from this point forward. If you do nothing today, then your past will be the best determinate of your future and future results. Stop doing the same thing and expecting different results! Stop being angry at God, and the world for your life being the way it is. It's your doing or the lack of your doing anything that holds the key! Face the fear, push through the resistance! Slay your dragons one at a time. Throw your foot over the boat of fear and step into your greatness! BE BOLD... BE BRAVE... BE GREAT!

Once I finished the 800 km Camino de Santiago in one month, I knew I had two months left. What would I do? I decided to walk 1200 more miles throughout 14 European countries because my walk wasn't over! My boots hit soil in Germany, Czech Republic, Hungary, Poland, Slovania, Slovakia, Austria, Herznagovia / Bosnia, Croatia, Belgium, Ireland, Iceland, France and Spain! This extended journey will be shared in my next book; until then, don't look for God in others, don't spend your time analyzing humanity! Instead, focus on your own walk and walk big and talk small! If you want to see God in the walks of others, then YOU WALK GOD... if you want to see goodness in humanity, then YOU WALK GOODNESS, compassion and love! If each person were to focus on walking the best they can; the world would change without choice!

Dear God, Thank You for loving me and seeing me as worthy even when the world didn't. Thank You for sending the angels throughout my life, that not only checked on me during dark hours but who lifted me up, encouraged me and walked your love not just talked it! Please help me to be a walking example of Your love, grace, mercy, compassion and tenderness; always looking at others through the eyes of Jesus touching them with His touch, speaking as He would speak to them, praying for others as He prayed for those that hurt him and serve as He served. Thank You for your sacrifice; being your daughter, makes me significant!

St. James, I've found peace, forgiveness, solitude, hope, health and so much more along your pilgrim paths and now I can only pray for those who come after, as I continue to walk big and talk big! Your whispers continue to bid for my return, hopefully hand in hand with my beloved Tom.

The world can change; one person at a time and it all begins with an interruption in one man's thinking! I pray this book has been your interruption and you're having a thought revival!

NOT the end…

merely the beginning…

of your

WALK TO BE REMEMBERED !

www.ingramcontent.com/pod-product-compliance
Lightning Source LLC
LaVergne TN
LVHW051541070426
835507LV00021B/2363